The Law of Play

Understanding Legalities in the Gaming Industry

Quinten J. Tenley

Copyright © 2024 by Quinten J. Tenley

All rights reserved.

No portion of this book may be reproduced in any form without written permission from the publisher or author, except as permitted by U.S. copyright law.

This publication is designed to provide accurate and authoritative information in regard to the subject matter covered. It is sold with the understanding that neither the author nor the publisher is engaged in rendering legal, investment, accounting or other professional services. While the publisher and author have used their best efforts in preparing this book, they make no representations or warranties with respect to the accuracy or completeness of the contents of this book and specifically disclaim any implied warranties of merchantability or fitness for a particular purpose. No warranty may be created or extended by sales representatives or written sales materials. The advice and strategies contained herein may not be suitable for your situation. You should consult with a professional when appropriate. Neither the publisher nor the author shall be liable for any loss of profit or any other commercial damages, including but not limited to special, incidental, consequential, personal, or other damages.

Contents

Introduction	1
1. The Foundations of Gaming Law	7
2. Licensing and Compliance	22
3. Intellectual Property Rights in Gaming	37
4. Player Rights and Consumer Protection	52
5. Monetization Models and Legal Ramifications	67
6. The Impact of Technology on Gaming Law	83
7. eSports and Competitive Gaming Law	99
8. Global Gaming and Cross-Border Regulations	115
9. Ethics, Morality, and Social Responsibility	131
10. Future Legal Challenges in Gaming	147
Conclusion	163

Introduction

The gaming industry has become a powerful cultural force, connecting billions of people across diverse backgrounds through digital entertainment, competition, and shared virtual experiences. Once confined to arcades and consoles, the gaming world has expanded into a massive, dynamic landscape encompassing everything from complex, immersive video games to the high-stakes world of online gambling, eSports, and virtual currencies. Today's gaming sector is a multibillion-dollar industry and an evolving ecosystem that demands comprehensive legal frameworks and regulations to address complex compliance, consumer protection, and emerging technologies. As gaming continues to grow and shift in form and function, so does the urgency for a clear understanding of the legalities that govern it. *The Law of Play: Understanding Legalities in the Gaming Industry* is designed to provide that critical knowledge.

At its core, this book explores the intricate network of laws, regulations, and ethical considerations that shape the gaming industry today. From content creation and distribution to intellectual property rights, licensing, consumer protection, and even the moral questions surrounding the design and monetization of games, each element is woven into a larger fabric of compliance and risk. As the industry increasingly overlaps with gambling due to monetization models like loot boxes, in-app purchases, and virtual currencies, the lines between gaming and gambling laws blur.

This intersection has created a minefield of legal issues that developers, publishers, investors, and players must carefully navigate. This book aims to demystify these legal complexities, clarifying the rights, responsibilities, and potential pitfalls facing anyone involved in the gaming industry.

The Rise of a New Legal Frontier

Historically, gaming regulations were designed for traditional forms of gambling like casinos, lotteries, and sports betting. With the rapid growth of digital gaming and the integration of advanced technologies such as artificial intelligence, virtual reality, and blockchain, these existing regulations often prove outdated and inadequate. Today's laws governing the industry were not necessarily designed to anticipate the rise of virtual economies, immersive experiences, and decentralized platforms. As new gaming and monetization models emerge, the legal landscape has had to adapt—and, in many cases, struggle to keep up.

For players, the concern may be transparency, fair play, and protection against exploitative practices. For businesses, legal considerations might revolve around securing intellectual property, preventing data breaches, or understanding licensing requirements across borders. For society, there are deeper moral questions about gambling addiction, age restrictions, and the responsibilities of gaming companies to provide safe, inclusive, and non-exploitative spaces. Thus, the gaming industry stands at a legal crossroads, where the evolution of law is as necessary as the evolution of technology.

Why Legal Knowledge Matters in Gaming

At its essence, gaming law serves as a regulatory framework to balance innovation with accountability, offering legal safeguards that protect stakeholders across the board. This knowledge is essential for developers and publishers to avoid costly legal disputes, protect their intellectual property, and ensure compliance with regional and international laws. For investors, a clear grasp of legal obligations and risks can make or break ventures in this rapidly fluctuating field. Understanding their rights can empower players to make informed decisions, resist unfair practices, and hold companies accountable.

As gaming companies seek to reach global audiences, they face the unique challenge of navigating varying and sometimes conflicting laws across different countries. Legal standards that apply in one jurisdiction may be nonexistent or even contradictory in another. This creates a regulatory complexity that can lead to financial loss or reputational damage if not managed correctly. By providing clarity on these issues, this book aims to equip readers with the tools and understanding to navigate a gaming landscape that is as legally intricate as it is innovative.

Exploring Key Issues: From Licensing to Emerging Technologies

Each chapter of this book delves into a specific area of gaming law, starting with the foundations of regulatory structures and progressing through more specialized topics such as intellectual property, licensing, consumer rights, and the burgeoning impact of technology. We'll cover the essentials of licensing and compliance for game publishers and online gaming operators and the significant role that intellectual property rights play in protecting creative assets and digital content.

A major focus of this book is on the monetization models within games, which have introduced a new array of legal and ethical challenges. Microtransactions, loot boxes, and in-app purchases have become ubiquitous, drawing criticism and regulatory scrutiny for their resemblance to gambling practices. Internationally, countries like Belgium and Japan have taken bold stances, either banning certain practices or imposing stringent regulations, while others have adopted a more lenient approach. As a result, the gaming industry faces a fragmented legal environment that adds another layer of complexity for companies seeking a global presence.

Emerging technologies such as blockchain, artificial intelligence, and virtual reality are rapidly reshaping the industry, raising questions about ownership, privacy, and accountability. Blockchain-based games, for example, create digital assets that hold real-world value, making them vulnerable to theft, fraud, and regulatory scrutiny. Similarly, virtual reality games introduce new dimensions of immersion that can lead to issues around user safety, personal data protection, and the mental health implications of extended play. In addressing these issues, we aim to provide a well-rounded understanding of the multifaceted legal and ethical landscape of gaming in the modern era.

A Holistic View of Gaming Law: Ethics, Responsibility, and the Future

As we dissect the law, this book also encourages a holistic view of gaming's role in society and the responsibilities that accompany it. From the ethics of game design to companies' accountability in preventing gambling addiction and protecting children, the gaming industry is under increased pressure to adopt ethical practices. This book does not merely outline the legal requirements; it seeks to foster a broader understanding of the social and ethical dimensions that influence regulatory actions and public perception.

The gaming industry is also poised to play a critical role in shaping future technologies and entertainment formats, from the rise of the metaverse to the use of artificial intelligence in immersive storytelling. While exciting, these innovations also bring potential risks, and the laws governing these spaces will likely evolve rapidly in the coming years. In this sense, gaming law is not a static field but a constantly evolving frontier where innovation meets regulation. The goal of this book is to equip readers not only with the knowledge of current laws but also with the foresight to anticipate and adapt to future challenges.

Navigating *The Law of Play*

Whether you are a game developer, a legal professional, an investor, or an avid gamer interested in understanding the industry's complexities, *The Law of Play* is here to provide insights and guidance. This book will help you make informed decisions, anticipate regulatory shifts, and grasp the foundational principles that define gaming law in the digital age. Together, we'll explore the laws, ethics, and social responsibilities that underpin one of the world's most influential industries, ensuring that all players—whether they're companies or consumers—understand the legal rules of the game.

Welcome to *The Law of Play*. Let's begin.

Chapter One

The Foundations of Gaming Law

The legal landscape of the gaming industry can seem intimidating, but understanding its foundations is essential. You'll find that differentiating between gaming and gambling is just the tip of the iceberg. Local, national, and international regulations shape the environment developers and operators must navigate. As technology evolves, so do the laws that govern these activities, often leading to complex compliance challenges. What implications do these shifting legal frameworks have for the future of gaming?

Overview of gaming and gambling regulations

Gaming and gambling regulations play an essential role in shaping the gaming industry's landscape. These regulations establish the legal framework within which all gaming activities operate, ensuring fairness, safety, and integrity for operators and players.

Regulations vary considerably across jurisdictions, reflecting different societal values and economic objectives. In some regions, regulators endeavor to promote responsible gaming while generating tax revenue, while others focus heavily on consumer protection and fraud prevention.

You should also recognize that the regulatory environment is constantly evolving. Emerging technologies, such as online gaming and blockchain, have prompted lawmakers to adapt or create new regulations. This adaptability is vital for maintaining a balance between fostering innovation and ensuring player safety.

For instance, many jurisdictions have implemented licensing requirements and age verification processes to prevent underage gambling and protect vulnerable populations.

Moreover, compliance with these regulations isn't optional; it's necessary for operators. Non-compliance can lead to severe penalties, including hefty fines or loss of licenses, which can threaten a business's viability.

As an operator or player, understanding these regulations can provide insights into how the gaming environment operates and the importance of ethical practices.

Differentiating gaming from gambling

Understanding the distinction between gaming and gambling is vital for managing the industry's complexities. While both activities involve play, they operate under fundamentally different principles.

Gaming refers to interactive entertainment that requires skill, strategy, or a combination of both. Whether playing video games, tabletop RPGs, or competitive eSports, the focus is engagement and mastery of the game mechanics. The outcome is often influenced by the player's decisions, making it a pursuit of skill and creativity.

On the other hand, gambling is primarily about wagering money on uncertain outcomes, where chance plays a significant role. In gambling, you're betting on results that are largely beyond your control, such as the roll of dice or the spin of a roulette wheel. The primary objective is to win money or prizes, which introduces regulatory scrutiny and legal implications that gaming typically doesn't face.

This distinction is significant, as it influences how laws are crafted and enforced. For instance, gaming might enjoy more lenient regulations compared to gambling, which is often tightly controlled due to concerns about addiction and financial implications.

Understanding these differences helps you navigate legal frameworks and informs business strategies and marketing approaches within the industry. Recognizing the nuances between gaming and gambling enables you to engage with stakeholders, regulators, and consumers, ensuring compliance and fostering a responsible gaming environment.

The role of local, national, and international laws

Maneuvering the landscape of gaming law requires awareness of local, national, and international regulations that shape the industry. Each jurisdiction has its own set of rules that govern gaming activities, which can vary greatly.

Local laws often dictate the licensing requirements for game developers and operators, which can influence the types of games available in your area. Understanding these local nuances is essential for compliance and can determine the success of your gaming venture.

At the national level, laws can vary widely, reflecting differing cultural attitudes towards gaming. For instance, the United States has a patchwork of regulations, with individual states determining their gaming policies. This fragmentation can create challenges for developers seeking a uniform approach across multiple markets.

Conversely, nations like the U.K. have more centralized regulations that streamline the process for gaming companies.

Treaties and agreements can further complicate the regulatory framework internationally. As you expand your reach, you'll need to navigate laws that govern cross-border gaming.

Countries like Malta and Gibraltar have become hubs for gaming companies due to their favorable regulatory environments, while others maintain stringent restrictions.

Regulatory authorities and their powers

Maneuvering the complexities of gaming law involves recognizing the significant role of regulatory authorities and their powers. These entities serve as the backbone of the gaming industry, guaranteeing compliance with laws and protecting the interests of consumers, operators, and the public.

Regulative authorities have a broad range of responsibilities, including licensing, oversight, enforcement, and the establishment of industry standards.

In your dealings within the gaming sector, it's vital to understand how these authorities operate. They possess the power to issue licenses to gaming operators, which serves as a gatekeeping mechanism to guarantee that only qualified entities can participate in the market. This licensing process often involves rigorous background checks, financial assessments, and examinations of operational practices.

Moreover, regulatory authorities monitor ongoing compliance, conducting audits and investigations to address potential violations. When non-compliance occurs, these bodies have the authority to impose penalties, including fines, suspensions, or even license revocations. This enforcement power is essential for maintaining integrity within the industry.

Furthermore, regulatory authorities often collaborate with law enforcement agencies to combat illegal gaming operations and fraud. Their influence extends beyond just enforcement; they shape policy by developing regulations that adapt to evolving technologies and market trends.

As you navigate the gaming landscape, recognizing the scope and impact of these regulatory bodies will be fundamental to your understanding of gaming law and its practical implications.

Evolution of gaming laws over time

The landscape of gaming laws has undergone significant changes over the years, reflecting shifts in societal attitudes, technological advancements, and economic considerations. Initially, gaming was heavily stigmatized and often outlawed in many jurisdictions.

However, as public perception began to evolve, particularly in the latter half of the 20th century, many governments recognized the potential for taxation and economic growth associated with regulated gaming. This shift led to the legalization of various forms of gambling, including casinos and lotteries.

As technology advanced, particularly with the rise of the internet, the gaming industry faced new challenges. Online gaming emerged, prompting jurisdictions to reevaluate existing laws. You might remember the debates surrounding the legality of online poker and sports betting, which necessitated the creation of new regulatory frameworks.

This evolution wasn't uniform; different regions adopted varied approaches, resulting in a patchwork of regulations.

In recent years, mobile gaming and esports have further complicated the legal landscape. You've likely noticed how these developments have spurred discussions about intellectual property rights, consumer protection, and age restrictions.

Governments are increasingly challenged to balance innovation with regulation, ensuring safety and fairness while promoting growth in a rapidly changing environment.

Common legal challenges in gaming industries

Numerous legal challenges confront the gaming industry today, stemming from the rapid evolution of technology and shifting regulatory landscapes.

One major challenge you might face is complying with diverse gaming regulations across different jurisdictions. Laws vary markedly from one region to another, making maneuvering through these regulations complex. If you operate online, consider how laws in different states or countries can impact your operations, often requiring you to adapt your business model to remain compliant.

Intellectual property (I.P.) issues also pose substantial challenges. As gaming technology advances, protecting your I.P. rights becomes increasingly vital. You'll need to guarantee that your game designs, characters, and narratives aren't only original and legally protected against infringement. Moreover, you may find it necessary to defend your creations against claims of copyright or patent violations.

Additionally, data privacy and security are ongoing concerns. With the rise of mobile and online gaming, you're likely collecting vast amounts of personal data from players. Compliance with laws like the General Data Protection Regulation (GDPR) in Europe or the California Consumer Privacy Act (CCPA) in the U.S. is essential. Breaching these laws can lead to severe penalties and damage your reputation.

Case studies: Landmark gaming law cases

In recent years, several landmark cases have shaped the landscape of gaming law, illustrating the industry's complexities and evolving nature. One notable case is United States v. McGowan, in which the Supreme Court ruled that state laws could impose regulations on tribal gaming operations. This case highlighted the tension between federal and state authorities and emphasized the need for clarity in jurisdictional boundaries.

Another notable case is *California v. Cabazon Band of Mission Indians*, which established that tribes aren't subject to state gaming regulations if those regulations don't apply to similar non-tribal gaming operations. This landmark decision reinforced the sovereignty of tribal nations in the gaming sector, compelling states to reassess their approach to regulation.

Additionally, the *Murphy v. National Collegiate Athletic Association* case led to the repeal of the Professional and Amateur Sports Protection Act (PASPA). This ruling allowed states to legalize sports betting, markedly reshaping the gaming landscape across the country. It illustrated the judiciary's role in promoting market accessibility while addressing the legal intricacies of sports gambling.

These cases show how judicial interpretation of existing laws can notably influence the gaming industry. Each ruling addressed immediate legal concerns and set precedents that continue to affect how gaming laws evolve.

As you navigate the complexities of gaming law, understanding these landmark cases is essential for grasping the legal landscape in which the gaming industry operates.

Policy development for fair play and safety

While gaming laws have evolved considerably, developing policies that guarantee fair play and safety remains essential for fostering trust within the industry. These policies serve as a framework to confirm that players have a level playing field, free from fraud and unfair practices. By establishing clear guidelines, stakeholders can promote transparency, which is imperative for maintaining player confidence in gaming platforms.

One critical aspect of policy development is integrating responsible gaming practices. You should consider how these policies encourage operators to implement features that help players manage their gaming habits, such as self-exclusion tools and deposit limits. This protects players and cultivates a responsible image for the industry, enhancing its reputation.

Moreover, safety protocols must address data protection and cybersecurity. Gaming companies handle sensitive personal information, so implementing robust data security measures is non-negotiable. Policies should mandate regular audits and compliance checks to confirm that data remains secure from breaches.

In addition, incorporating player feedback into policy development can lead to more effective regulations. Actively engaging with the gaming community allows you to understand their concerns and expectations, ultimately leading to policies that reflect their needs.

The moral and ethical dimensions of gaming laws

The intersection of morality and ethics in gaming laws is essential for shaping an industry that prioritizes player welfare and social responsibility. As you navigate this landscape, it's important to recognize how these dimensions influence regulations and gaming culture.

Ethical considerations compel lawmakers to evaluate the potential harm that games may pose, especially to vulnerable populations. This includes addressing issues like addiction, violence, and exploitation, which can greatly impact players' lives and society at large.

When creating content, you might consider the responsibility of game developers and publishers. Ethical gaming laws encourage transparency regarding in-game mechanics, such as loot boxes or microtransactions, which can mislead or exploit players. By imposing laws that demand clear disclosures, the industry fosters a culture of accountability and builds trust with its audience.

Moreover, diversity and inclusion are critical facets of morality in gaming. Laws that promote equitable representation can lead to richer narratives and more relatable experiences for players. When you advocate for inclusive policies, you're not just complying with legal standards but also championing a healthier gaming environment that values all voices.

Ultimately, gaming laws' moral and ethical dimensions aren't just theoretical. They shape the industry's practices and can guide meaningful change. By understanding these principles, you can actively contribute to a gaming culture that prioritizes ethical considerations and enhances player experiences.

Role of lobbying and advocacy in gaming law

Lobbying and advocacy play essential roles in shaping gaming laws and influencing the regulatory landscape to reflect the interests of various stakeholders. As someone involved in this industry, you must understand how these efforts can directly impact legislation governing gaming operations, taxation, and consumer protections.

Key players in gaming law, such as casino operators, game developers, and advocacy groups, often employ lobbyists to push for favorable regulations and mitigate restrictions. These lobbyists engage with lawmakers, presenting data and narratives that support their positions. Successful lobbying efforts can lead to more permissive gaming laws, which not only benefit the companies involved but can also enhance local economies through job creation and increased tax revenue.

Moreover, advocacy groups focused on responsible gaming and consumer protection also play an important role. They work to guarantee that laws are designed with the public's best interest in mind, advocating for regulations that promote safe gaming environments. This duality of interest—where commercial gains meet consumer welfare—highlights the complexity of gaming law.

You must recognize that the effectiveness of lobbying and advocacy can vary notably, depending on the political climate and public sentiment. Engaging in these activities requires a nuanced understanding of the legal framework and socio-economic factors.

Ultimately, the interplay between lobbying and advocacy shapes the future of gaming law, creating a dynamic environment that continually evolves to meet new challenges and opportunities.

The impact of public perception on legislation

Public perception greatly shapes legislation surrounding gaming laws, influencing how lawmakers approach regulatory changes. When society views gaming positively, it often leads to more progressive legislation, such as the legalization of sports betting or online gambling. Conversely, if gaming is seen negatively—associated with addiction or crime—lawmakers may impose stricter regulations or even ban certain practices. This dynamic underscores the significance of public sentiment in shaping legal frameworks.

You might notice that various factors often influence public perception, including media portrayal, advocacy groups, and public incidents. For example, sensational news stories about gambling addiction can spark fear and lead to calls for stricter regulations. Lawmakers, keen to respond to constituents' concerns, may then introduce legislation that reflects those fears, regardless of the actual statistical data on gambling-related issues.

Social media has amplified this effect, as public opinion can shift rapidly. A viral post highlighting a negative gaming aspect can lead to immediate legislative discussions, pushing lawmakers to act swiftly. Additionally, grassroots movements can mobilize community members, making it essential for lawmakers to evaluate public sentiment before drafting or amending laws.

Ultimately, understanding the interplay between public perception and legislation is vital for anyone in the gaming industry. By remaining aware of societal attitudes and trends, you can better navigate the often-complex landscape of gaming law and anticipate potential regulatory changes that could affect your interests.

Cultural and societal differences in gaming regulation

Recognizing the cultural and societal differences in gaming regulation is essential for understanding the varied legal landscapes worldwide. Each nation's approach to gaming law is shaped by its unique historical, cultural, and social contexts. For instance, gaming is often intertwined with cultural traditions in countries like Japan, leading to stringent regulations that preserve local customs.

In contrast, the United States showcases a more liberal stance, with state-level regulations allowing for diverse gaming experiences and innovations.

Consider how societal attitudes toward gambling influence regulatory frameworks. In some regions, gaming is viewed as a harmful vice, leading to rigorous restrictions to protect citizens. In others, it's celebrated as entertainment, fostering an environment where gaming thrives and evolves. This divergence can lead to different legal standards, from age restrictions to advertising regulations.

Moreover, the role of technology exacerbates these differences. Countries with advanced technological infrastructure often adapt more quickly to online gaming, while those with less access may lag behind. This challenges international gaming companies attempting to navigate a patchwork of regulations.

Understanding these cultural and societal nuances is vital for anyone involved in the gaming industry. It informs compliance with local laws and shapes strategic decisions, marketing approaches, and community engagement efforts.

Globalization and cross-border gaming law conflicts

As globalization continues to reshape the gaming industry, conflicts arising from cross-border gaming laws pose significant challenges for operators and regulators alike. The rapid expansion of online gaming platforms means you'll likely encounter varying legal frameworks across jurisdictions. Each country has its own set of regulations, and compliance becomes increasingly complex when your operations span multiple borders.

One of the most pressing issues you'll face is the legal definition and standard inconsistency. For instance, what's deemed acceptable in one country may be prohibited in another, leading to potential legal jeopardy. You're often caught in conflicting obligations, complicating your business strategies.

Additionally, enforcement becomes a challenge; regulatory authorities may have limited power over foreign operators, which can lead to non-compliance.

Moreover, the rise of virtual currencies and blockchain technology adds another layer of complexity. These innovations mightn't be uniformly regulated, creating a patchwork of laws you must navigate. Understanding these nuances is vital to avoid hefty fines and reputational damage if you're operating in multiple jurisdictions.

As you grapple with these challenges, it is important to stay informed about international treaties, regional agreements, and emerging frameworks that aim to streamline gaming regulations. Engaging with legal experts specializing in cross-border gaming law can also help mitigate risks and maintain compliance.

Adapting to this dynamic landscape isn't just about following the law; it's about strategically positioning your business for success in an increasingly interconnected world.

Foundations of online gaming laws

The complexities of cross-border gaming law underscore the importance of understanding the foundational principles of online gaming laws. As you navigate this intricate landscape, you must grasp the regulatory frameworks governing online gaming activities. These laws vary greatly across jurisdictions, with some countries embracing online gaming and others imposing strict prohibitions.

Licensing is one of the core components of online gaming laws. Most jurisdictions require operators to obtain licenses, ensuring compliance with local regulations and promoting consumer protection. These licensing requirements often dictate aspects like game types, payout ratios, and responsible gambling measures.

Another significant aspect to consider is taxation. Many regions impose taxes on gaming revenue, which can influence operators' business models. Understanding these tax obligations is crucial for any operator to maintain compliance and profitability.

Consumer protection laws also play an essential role. Regulations typically mandate that operators implement safeguards to protect players from fraud, addiction, and unfair gaming practices. This involves transparent terms and conditions, secure payment methods, and accessible customer support.

Legal definitions and terminology in gaming

Understanding legal definitions and terminology in gaming is essential for anyone involved in the industry, whether you're an operator, player, or regulator. Familiarity with specific terms can considerably influence navigating legal landscapes and compliance requirements.

For instance, "gambling" often encompasses betting, wagering, and staking, but its legal interpretation can vary by jurisdiction.

Terms like "skill-based games" and "chance-based games" carry distinct implications. In many regions, skill-based games may escape the stringent regulations that govern chance-based activities, affecting their marketing and operation.

Similarly, understanding what constitutes "illegal gaming" can help you identify activities that may expose you to legal risks.

You'll also encounter terms like "licensing," "regulatory body," and "compliance," which are critical for operators seeking to establish a lawful presence in the market. Each jurisdiction has its own licensing requirements; failing to understand these can result in hefty fines or operational shutdowns.

Additionally, concepts like "player protection" and "responsible gaming" are increasingly relevant as regulators focus on safeguarding participants and promoting ethical practices.

These terms highlight the industry's shift toward prioritizing consumer welfare, which you must consider in your operations and strategies.

Chapter Two

Licensing and Compliance

When you consider entering the gaming industry, licensing and compliance aren't just buzzwords; they're essential for success. Steering through the intricate web of regulations can feel intimidating, especially with the varying standards across regions. You must understand how to secure a gaming license and the implications of failing to comply with legal requirements. With the high stakes, what happens if you overlook these vital elements? The answers might surprise you, prompting you to reconsider your approach to this dynamic field.

Importance of licensing in gaming operations

In the gaming industry, licensing serves as a critical foundation for operational legitimacy and consumer trust. Without a proper license, your gaming operation risks being viewed as untrustworthy, which can deter potential players and partners. Licensing legitimizes your business and guarantees adherence to local and international regulations designed to protect consumers and maintain fair play.

When you obtain a gaming license, you commit to operating within a framework that includes compliance with stringent regulatory standards. These standards often cover game fairness, data protection, and responsible gaming practices. Doing so demonstrates your dedication to ethical operations, which can greatly enhance your brand's reputation.

Moreover, a valid gaming license safeguards against potential legal issues. Should disputes arise, having a license indicates that you're operating within the law, offering protection. This can facilitate smoother interactions with banking institutions and payment processors, who often prefer or require licensed operators.

Licensing can also create a competitive advantage. In a crowded market, being a licensed operator can set you apart from unlicensed competitors. Players are more likely to trust and choose your platform over others that lack regulatory oversight.

Lastly, the dynamic nature of the gaming industry means that regulations can evolve. A solid licensing framework helps you remain compliant today and prepares you for future regulatory changes, guaranteeing your operation's longevity and success.

Steps to obtain a gaming license

Securing a gaming license involves several essential steps that guarantee compliance with regulatory requirements. First, you must identify the regulatory authority governing gaming in your jurisdiction. Each region has its rules, so understanding these is imperative for your application process.

Next, prepare your business plan, ensuring it aligns with local laws. This plan should detail your gaming operations, including the types of games you'll offer, your target market, and your financial projections. You must also outline your compliance strategy, demonstrating your commitment to responsible gaming and customer protection.

After drafting your business plan, gather all necessary documentation. This typically includes proof of identity for all owners and key personnel, financial statements, and any relevant background checks. Be meticulous in this stage, as incomplete applications can lead to delays or denials.

Once your documentation is ready, submit your application and the required fees. Regulatory bodies often conduct rigorous reviews, so be prepared for potential interviews or additional inquiries. During this phase, transparency is essential; discrepancies can jeopardize your chances of obtaining a license.

Lastly, once granted, maintain ongoing compliance. This means keeping your operations within regulatory guidelines, submitting periodic reports, and being ready for inspections.

Key differences in licensing by region

Understanding the key differences in gaming licensing by region is vital for operators aiming to navigate the complex landscape of regulatory compliance. Each jurisdiction has distinct requirements, processes, and types of licenses that can greatly impact your operations.

For instance, countries like the UK and Malta offer detailed frameworks in Europe, emphasizing player protection and responsible gaming. The UK Gambling Commission requires extensive documentation, including proof of financial stability and adherence to social responsibility measures. At the same time, Malta's regulatory body promotes an accessible licensing process but demands transparency in operations.

In contrast, jurisdictions like the United States present a patchwork of regulations, where each state has its own licensing requirements. For example, New Jersey's Division of Gaming Enforcement mandates rigorous background checks and detailed financial disclosures, reflecting its commitment to consumer protection. Meanwhile, states like Nevada have long-standing regulatory structures prioritizing innovation and compliance, attracting diverse gaming operators.

Asia also showcases varied approaches. Countries like Singapore implement strict regulations to maintain high standards, while others like the Philippines have developed more lenient frameworks to encourage foreign investments.

Understanding these regional variances in licensing is essential for compliance and strategic decision-making regarding market entry, operational scalability, and risk management. Recognizing these differences can better position your business to thrive in the competitive global gaming market.

Major licensing bodies worldwide

Maneuvering the complexities of gaming regulation requires familiarity with the major licensing bodies worldwide. These organizations are vital in guaranteeing that gaming operations adhere to the established legal frameworks, maintaining integrity and fairness within the industry.

In North America, the Nevada Gaming Control Board (NGCB) stands out as a pivotal authority, regulating all aspects of gaming in Nevada. Similarly, in Canada, provincial regulators such as the Alcohol and Gaming Commission of Ontario (AGCO) oversee local gaming operations, enforcing compliance with both federal and provincial laws.

The United Kingdom Gambling Commission (UKGC) plays a significant role in Europe. It not only licenses operators but also enforces regulations to protect consumers and guarantee fair play. Other European countries have their own regulatory bodies, such as the Malta Gaming

Authority (MGA), renowned for its proactive approach to compliance and innovation in gaming.

The regulatory landscape in Asia varies widely. The Philippine Amusement and Gaming Corporation (PAGCOR) oversees gaming in the Philippines, while in Macau, the Gaming Inspection and Coordination Bureau regulates the industry with stringent licensing requirements.

Understanding the functions and jurisdictions of these bodies is essential for any gaming operator. Each licensing body has specific criteria, processes, and ongoing compliance obligations that you must navigate.

Maintaining compliance with legal standards

Maneuvering through the maze of legal standards in the gaming industry demands vigilance and a proactive approach. You must stay informed about the specific regulations that apply to your operations, from licensing requirements to consumer protection laws. Each jurisdiction has its own legal framework; understanding these nuances is vital for compliance.

Regularly review the laws governing your business activities to guarantee adherence to current regulations.

Implementing a robust compliance program is essential. This involves establishing clear policies and procedures that align with legal standards. You should conduct regular audits and risk assessments to identify any areas of potential non-compliance. Documenting these processes reinforces your commitment to compliance and provides a roadmap for future reference.

Training your staff is equally important. Ascertain that they're well-versed in the legal obligations that pertain to their roles. A knowledgeable team can help mitigate risks associated with compliance failures.

Additionally, consider engaging with legal experts who specialize in gaming law. They can provide valuable insights and guidance tailored to your specific needs.

Addressing non-compliance consequences

Non-compliance in the gaming industry can lead to serious repercussions beyond financial penalties. When you fail to adhere to regulatory standards, you risk hefty fines and the potential loss of your operating license. This loss can result in the cessation of your business activities, disrupting your revenue stream and damaging your reputation within the industry.

Moreover, non-compliance can invite legal action from regulatory bodies or even civil lawsuits from consumers. Such legal entanglements can consume significant time and resources, diverting focus from your core operations.

The public perception of your brand can also suffer, as stakeholders and customers may lose trust in your ability to operate ethically and responsibly.

In addition, non-compliance can lead to stricter scrutiny from regulators in the future. Once you've been flagged for violations, expect more frequent audits and a heightened level of oversight.

This can complicate your operations and increase operational costs as you scramble to meet compliance standards.

Licensing in online vs. land-based gaming

In the gaming industry, licensing requirements differ greatly between online and land-based operations, each presenting unique challenges and regulatory landscapes.

For land-based gaming, you typically navigate a structured environment governed by local, state, or national regulations. These regulations often entail extensive background checks, financial disclosures, and adherence to specific operational standards. You'll need to acquire licenses from multiple authorities, which can vary considerably depending on your location. This process can be time-consuming and resource-intensive but provides a framework that guarantees compliance with established laws.

In contrast, regulatory bodies often issue online gaming licenses in jurisdictions known for their favorable gaming laws, such as Malta or Gibraltar. Here, the focus shifts toward digital compliance, including cybersecurity measures, responsible gaming protocols, and data protection regulations.

Online operators face additional hurdles related to cross-border regulations, as different countries impose varying restrictions on online gaming activities.

Moreover, the online landscape is rapidly evolving, influencing how licensing authorities approach compliance. You'll need to stay informed about the latest technological advancements and their implications for regulatory compliance. This may include adapting to new verification processes or guaranteeing that your gaming platform meets specific technical standards.

Emerging issues in licensing (e.g., blockchain)

As the gaming industry continues to evolve, new technologies like blockchain are introducing a range of emerging issues in licensing. These advancements create both opportunities and challenges that you must navigate carefully.

The decentralized nature of blockchain can complicate traditional licensing frameworks, which often rely on centralized authorities. Here are three key issues to reflect upon:

1. **Regulatory Compliance**: Blockchain-based gaming platforms may not fit neatly into existing regulatory frameworks. You'll need to determine how local and international laws apply to decentralized systems, ensuring compliance while maintaining blockchain's innovative edge.

2. **Ownership and IP Rights**: With the rise of non-fungible tokens (NFTs) and digital assets, questions about ownership and intellectual property rights arise. You must clearly define who owns the rights to in-game assets and how that ownership is transferred, ensuring that your licensing agreements are robust and enforceable.

3. **Consumer Protection**: As blockchain enables greater anonymity and decentralization, ensuring consumer protection becomes more complex. You'll need to establish dispute resolution and fraud prevention mechanisms, which can be challenging in a decentralized environment.

Navigating these emerging issues requires a proactive approach. To stay ahead in this dynamic landscape, you should conduct thorough research, engage with legal experts, and continuously monitor regulatory changes.

Embracing these challenges will help you remain compliant and enhance your competitive advantage in the gaming industry.

Legal challenges in self-regulated platforms

Self-regulated platforms often face significant legal challenges impacting their operation and reputation. While these platforms aim to create a controlled environment, they may encounter scrutiny from regulatory bodies due to their self-governing nature. One primary concern involves the adequacy of player protection measures. If you fail to implement robust safeguards against underage gambling or fraud, you could face severe penalties and damage your credibility in the industry.

Another challenge arises from the ambiguity in compliance standards. You might find that your self-regulatory framework doesn't align with evolving legal expectations, leading to conflicts with state or national laws. This misalignment can expose you to litigation or regulatory intervention, disrupting your operations and resulting in costly legal battles.

Moreover, self-regulated platforms must contend with varying interpretations of laws across jurisdictions. If your platform operates internationally, you're likely to encounter a patchwork of regulations that complicate compliance efforts. Failing to navigate these complexities can lead to serious repercussions, including fines or operational shutdowns.

Additionally, the lack of transparency in self-regulation can raise red flags for players and regulators. If you can't demonstrate accountability and adherence to ethical standards, users might question the integrity of your platform, potentially leading to decreased user trust and engagement.

Compliance audits and their role

Compliance audits ensure that gaming platforms adhere to established regulations and maintain operational integrity.

These audits systematically evaluate a platform's adherence to applicable laws, helping to identify areas that require improvement or correction.

By conducting regular audits, you mitigate risks and enhance the overall credibility of your operations.

Here are three key aspects of compliance audits in the gaming industry:

1. **Regulatory Adherence**: Compliance audits assess whether your gaming platform meets all relevant regulations. This includes examining licensing requirements, age verification processes, and advertising standards.

By ensuring compliance, you avoid potential legal penalties and maintain your license.

2. **Operational Efficiency**: Audits help identify operational inefficiencies. You can streamline operations, reduce costs, and improve overall performance by analyzing processes and controls.

An efficient platform attracts more users and retains them by providing a secure and reliable gaming experience.

3. **Risk Management**: Regular audits are critical in identifying and managing risks. By pinpointing vulnerabilities, you can implement corrective measures before issues escalate.

This proactive approach protects your business and builds trust with regulators and players alike.

Financial transparency and anti-money laundering

Financial transparency and anti-money laundering (AML) measures in the gaming industry are crucial for maintaining trust and integrity. By implementing robust AML protocols, you protect your business from illicit activities and enhance your reputation among players and stakeholders.

Regulators mandate that you establish clear policies, conduct regular audits, and maintain thorough records of all transactions to guarantee compliance with AML laws.

You must identify and verify customers through Know Your Customer (KYC) processes, which involve collecting personal information and evaluating the risk of money laundering. This proactive approach allows you to detect suspicious activities early and report them to the relevant authorities.

Additionally, fostering a culture of transparency within your organization cultivates a responsible gaming environment and reassures your clientele that their financial interactions are secure.

Your compliance with AML regulations safeguards your operations and contributes to the overall health of the gaming ecosystem. Adhering to financial transparency principles deter criminal enterprises from exploiting your platform.

It is crucial to train your employees to recognize red flags associated with money laundering, such as unusual betting patterns or large cash transactions.

The impact of GDPR on gaming compliance

As gaming companies enhance their financial transparency and anti-money laundering protocols, they must also navigate the complexities introduced by the General Data Protection Regulation (GDPR). This regulation fundamentally shifts how you handle player data, and compliance is non-negotiable if you wish to avoid hefty fines and reputational damage.

Here are three significant aspects you should consider:
1. **Data Minimization**: Under GDPR, you are required to collect only the data necessary for your purposes. This means you need to evaluate your data collection practices and guarantee that you are not overstepping boundaries by gathering excessive information.

2. **User Consent**: It is vital to gain explicit consent from players before processing their data. You must establish clear, understandable consent forms and guarantee players can easily withdraw their consent anytime. This transparency builds trust and aligns with regulatory requirements.

3. **Data Security**: You're responsible for implementing robust security measures to protect player data from breaches. This includes encryption, regular audits, and employee training on data protection protocols. Failure to safeguard personal information can lead to severe penalties under GDPR.

Navigating these regulations isn't just about compliance; it's about fostering a responsible gaming environment.

Gaming taxes and how they vary by jurisdiction

Gaming taxes represent a notable regulatory challenge that varies widely by jurisdiction, impacting gaming companies' operational strategies. Each region establishes its tax framework, which can include varying rates on revenue, prizes, or specific gaming activities. For instance, some states impose a flat tax on gross gaming revenue, while others utilize a tiered structure that escalates based on earnings. This variation necessitates a thorough understanding of local tax obligations for companies operating in multiple jurisdictions.

In addition to the rates themselves, the timing and method of tax collection can differ. Some jurisdictions require upfront payments or deposits, while others may impose taxes quarterly or annually. Companies must guarantee compliance with these schedules to avoid penalties, which can considerably affect cash flow and operational planning.

Moreover, gaming taxes have implications beyond immediate financial obligations. They can influence market entry strategies, pricing models, and even the choice of gaming platforms. Companies must remain vigilant about changes in local legislation, as tax rates can fluctuate based on political climates or economic conditions.

Navigating this complex landscape requires a robust accounting system and strategic legal counsel to interpret and comply with varying regulations. Gaming companies can mitigate risks and enhance their competitive positioning within the industry by prioritizing compliance and understanding these tax nuances.

Advertising and marketing compliance

Understanding the intricate landscape of gaming taxes leads directly to another significant regulatory concern: advertising and marketing compliance. In the gaming industry, you must be aware that your promotional activities aren't only subject to scrutiny and tightly regulated.

Guaranteeing compliance is vital, as missteps can lead to severe consequences, including hefty fines or even loss of your operating license.

To navigate this complex regulatory environment, keep these key considerations in mind:

1. **Truthfulness and Transparency**: Always provide clear and accurate information about your games, including odds, payouts, and rules. Misleading claims can result in legal actions from both regulators and consumers.

2. **Target Audience Restrictions**: Be mindful of who you're targeting with your advertisements. Many jurisdictions have strict rules about marketing to minors or vulnerable populations. As-

certain your campaigns are directed at appropriate demographics.

3. **Responsible Gaming Messaging**: Your marketing efforts should promote responsible gaming practices. This includes providing information on self-exclusion options and encouraging players to gamble within their means.

Risks of operating without proper licensing

Operating without proper licensing can expose your business to significant legal and financial risks, particularly in a heavily regulated industry like gaming.

Initially, engaging in operations without the necessary licenses can lead to hefty fines imposed by regulatory authorities. These fines can accumulate quickly, potentially crippling your financial standing and damaging your reputation.

Moreover, you risk facing civil lawsuits from players or competitors. If you're found to be operating illegally, you could be liable for damages, which may far exceed the initial investment in compliance. This scenario affects your resources and can deter future partnerships and investments, as potential collaborators often scrutinize licensing status before engaging with any business.

Additionally, you could lose access to critical payment processing services without proper licensing. Many banks and payment providers require licensing as a prerequisite for establishing accounts. If flagged as unlicensed, you may find it challenging to operate your business effectively, leading to cash flow issues and customer dissatisfaction.

Finally, the reputational damage incurred from non-compliance can be long-lasting. In an industry where trust is paramount, being labeled as unlicensed can alienate customers and erode loyalty.

Once trust is lost, regaining it can be an uphill battle, often requiring extensive marketing and outreach efforts.

Chapter Three

Intellectual Property Rights in Gaming

When you're steering through the gaming industry, understanding Intellectual Property Rights (IPR) isn't just beneficial; it's essential. These rights protect everything from innovative game mechanics to brands you recognize. You might think it's all about creativity, but a complex web of legalities can make or break a developer's success. As the landscape shifts with new technologies and platforms, the implications of IPR could greatly affect your next project. What happens when these rights clash, and how can you safeguard your creations?

Understanding IP rights and why they matter

Intellectual property (IP) rights play an essential role in the gaming industry, shaping how creators protect their innovations and ideas. Understanding IP rights is crucial for anyone involved in gaming, whether you're a developer, designer, or gamer.

These rights safeguard your creative output, allowing you to maintain control over your work and profit from it. Without IP protections, the risk of idea theft and unauthorized use skyrockets, undermining the hard work and investment you've put into your projects.

IP rights encompass various protections, including copyrights, trademarks, and trade secrets. Copyrights safeguard your game's code, art, and narrative, ensuring that others can't reproduce or distribute your work without permission.

Trademarks, however, protect the branding elements associated with your game, such as logos and character names, which help establish your game's identity in a crowded market. Trade secrets can cover unique processes or formulas that give your game a competitive edge.

These rights benefit creators and enrich the gaming ecosystem. By safeguarding innovations, you encourage a culture of creativity and originality.

This dynamic environment fosters competition, leading to better games and enhancing player experiences. So, if you're serious about your role in gaming, prioritize understanding IP rights.

They're not just legal niceties but crucial tools for protecting your creative vision and ensuring the sustainability of the industry you love.

Patents in gaming technology and mechanics

Patents are a critical mechanism for protecting innovative gaming technologies and mechanics, enabling developers to secure exclusive rights to their inventions. When you create a unique feature or technology within a game, applying for a patent can be your best defense against competition. It grants you the legal authority to exclude others from using, selling, or distributing your invention, ultimately allowing you to capitalize on your creativity and investment.

Patents can foster innovation in the fast-paced gaming industry, where trends shift rapidly. By securing your inventions, you encourage further development in the field; when developers know their ideas are protected, they're more likely to invest time and resources into creating groundbreaking technologies. This can lead to a cycle of innovation that benefits creators and consumers.

However, maneuvering the patent landscape can be complex. You must carefully assess whether your technology meets the criteria for patentability—novelty, non-obviousness, and utility. Failing to do so might result in wasted time and resources.

The patent application process can be time-consuming and costly, leading many developers to weigh the pros and cons of pursuing patents.

Ultimately, understanding and strategically utilizing gaming technology and mechanics patents can position you ahead of the competition. When you protect your innovations, you're not just safeguarding your work but also contributing to the broader evolution of the gaming industry.

Embracing patent rights is essential to ensuring your ideas thrive in a crowded marketplace.

Copyright law in game design and content

Protecting your creative assets is just as important as securing innovative technologies when developing a game. Copyright law plays an essential role in safeguarding the unique elements of your game, such as graphics, music, characters, and storyline. This legal framework grants you exclusive rights to your original works, allowing you to control their use and distribution. By understanding and leveraging copyright law, you can prevent unauthorized use of your creative content, which can greatly impact your game's success.

In the gaming industry, copyright protection automatically applies when creating an original work. However, registering your copyright with the U.S. Copyright Office—or the equivalent in your jurisdiction—provides added benefits, including the ability to sue for damages in case of infringement. This step is imperative for asserting your rights and deterring potential infringers from misusing your work.

Moreover, consider the implications of using third-party assets. If you incorporate music, artwork, or code created by others without permission, you risk facing legal challenges that could derail your project. Always verify you have the proper licenses or create original content.

Understanding copyright law protects you legally and enhances your game's marketability. It helps establish your brand as a creator who values originality and innovation. Ultimately, taking copyright seriously can make a considerable difference in your game's longevity and your reputation in the industry.

Trademarks and brand protection in gaming

In the competitive gaming landscape, securing trademarks is essential for protecting your brand identity and ensuring consumer recognition. Trademarks distinguish your names, logos, and characters, creating a unique identity that distinguishes you from competitors. This differentiation is vital because consumers often make purchasing decisions based on brand recognition. If you don't actively protect your trademarks, you risk diluting your brand and potential confusion among consumers.

Establishing strong trademark protections safeguards your creations and enhances your market position. Registering your trademarks gives you exclusive rights to use these marks in commerce, which can translate into significant financial advantages. This exclusivity is invaluable in an industry where brand loyalty can drive sales.

Moreover, effective trademark management goes beyond mere registration. You need to actively monitor the market for potential infringements. This vigilance helps you swiftly address unauthorized uses of your trademarks, preventing others from capitalizing on your hard work and creativity.

Legal actions against infringers not only protect your brand but also serve as a deterrent to future violations.

Licensing vs. ownership in IP for gaming assets

Securing trademarks is just one aspect of managing intellectual property in the gaming industry; understanding the dynamics between licensing and ownership of gaming assets is equally important. When you create a game, you're not just developing a product but also generating a range of intellectual property rights.

Deciding whether to license these rights or retain ownership can greatly impact your project's success and future opportunities.

Ownership means you have full control over your intellectual property. You can capitalize on it however you see fit, whether through merchandise, sequels, or adaptations. However, ownership also comes with enforcement responsibility, which can be costly and time-consuming.

On the other hand, licensing allows you to share your IP with others, generating revenue without the burden of full ownership. This can be beneficial if you want to expand your brand through collaborations or partnerships.

But be cautious; licensing agreements can sometimes lead to control and revenue-sharing disputes. You'll want to negotiate terms that protect your interests while allowing creative collaboration.

Ultimately, the choice between licensing and ownership isn't just a legal decision; it's a strategic one that should align with your long-term goals. By weighing the benefits and drawbacks, you can make informed decisions that enhance your position in the gaming landscape, ensuring your creative vision is protected and profitable.

IP issues in game streaming and fan content

Maneuvering the IP issues surrounding game streaming and fan content can be complex, especially as the lines between creator and consumer blur.

As you engage in streaming or creating fan content, you must navigate several legal challenges that could impact your rights and the rights of others. Here are key considerations:

- **Copyright Ownership**: Understand who owns the game's content and what rights you have to use it.

- **Fair Use Doctrine**: Familiarize yourself with fair use principles, particularly how they apply to commentary, criticism, or educational content.

- **Licensing Agreements**: Know if you need a license to stream the game or use its assets in your content.

- **DMCA Takedown Notices**: If you use copyrighted material without permission, you may receive DMCA notices.

- **Monetization Implications**: Recognize how monetizing your content may affect your legal standing regarding IP rights.

These factors are significant for protecting yourself while contributing to the gaming community.

Many game developers support fan content, but not all are lenient. Some companies actively enforce their IP rights, which can lead to legal action against you.

Legal risks of game modding and hacking

Game modding and hacking can open up new experiences and extend the life of a game, but they come with significant legal risks that you should be aware of. The primary concern revolves around intellectual property (IP) rights. When you modify a game, you're often altering copyrighted material, which can lead to potential lawsuits from the original developers or publishers.

Even if you believe your mod is transformative, the legal precedent surrounding fair use in gaming remains murky.

Additionally, hacking can expose you to cybersecurity threats. Many hacks require you to download third-party software, which might contain malware or violate the game's terms of service. If you get caught using hacks, you risk account bans and legal action from the game companies.

Remember, companies like Blizzard and Valve have established a history of pursuing legal action against modders and hackers.

Moreover, distributing mods or hacks can amplify your legal exposure. Even if you've created something innovative, sharing it online can attract the ire of IP holders. They have the right to enforce their trademarks and copyrights vigorously, and your actions could be seen as infringing on their rights.

In short, while modding and hacking can enhance your gaming experience, weighing the potential legal ramifications is vital. Always consider whether the benefits outweigh the risks, and stay informed about the legal landscape in gaming to protect yourself from unintended consequences.

Protecting in-game assets and virtual property

Protecting your in-game assets and virtual property becomes vital when you invest time and money into a game.

The digital landscape is rife with threats that can undermine your experience and investment. Understanding how to safeguard your virtual items is essential for every gamer.

Here are some strategies to help you protect your in-game assets:

- **Use Strong Passwords**: Secure your gaming account with complex passwords to prevent unauthorized access.

- **Enable Two-Factor Authentication**: This adds an extra layer of protection, making it harder for hackers to compromise your account.

- **Stay Informed**: Keep up with the latest security updates from your game developers and platforms.

- **Be Cautious with Third-Party Services**: Avoid using unverified websites for trading or selling virtual items, as they may pose substantial risks.

- **Backup Your Data**: Regularly back up your game data to guarantee you don't lose your progress or assets.

Counterfeiting and copyright infringement

Counterfeiting and copyright infringement threaten the integrity of the gaming industry's creative landscape. Considering developers spend vast amounts of time and resources creating unique games, it becomes clear how damaging these violations can be.

Counterfeit games often mimic popular titles, luring unsuspecting players into purchasing subpar products. This dilutes the brand value of legitimate games and undermines consumer trust in the gaming market.

Copyright infringement, on the other hand, occurs when someone uses a game's assets—like characters, music, or storylines—without permission. This practice stifles innovation, as creators may hesitate to explore new ideas if they fear their work will be copied or misused.

You might think piracy is harmless, but it harms the entire ecosystem. Developers rely on revenues from game sales to fund future projects, and when piracy runs rampant, those funds dwindle.

Moreover, counterfeiting and copyright infringement can lead to legal battles that drain resources and distract from game development. For you as a player, this means fewer quality games and potentially higher prices as companies try to recover lost revenue.

It's crucial to support original creators by purchasing legitimate products. Doing so contributes to a healthier gaming environment where creativity can flourish.

Protecting intellectual property rights isn't just about legal compliance; it's about preserving the artistry and innovation that make gaming an exciting and vibrant industry.

Global IP issues and jurisdictional conflicts

As the gaming industry grapples with counterfeiting and copyright infringement, it also faces a complex web of global intellectual property (IP) issues and jurisdictional conflicts. Steering through these challenges isn't merely a matter of local laws; it requires understanding international frameworks and how they interact—or clash—with one another.

Key issues include:

- **Diverse IP Laws**: Different countries have varying standards for IP protection, leading to potential gaps in enforcement.

- **Enforcement Difficulties**: The digital nature of gaming complicates jurisdiction, making it hard to determine which laws apply.

- **Cross-Border Transactions**: Online sales and downloads often occur across borders, creating confusion over which legal system governs.

- **Cultural Differences**: What's considered fair use in one country may be a violation in another, complicating global distribution strategies.

- **Evolving Technology**: Rapid technological advancements outpace existing legal frameworks, resulting in outdated regulations.

Given these complexities, you need to be proactive in your approach. Understanding the nuances of IP rights in different jurisdictions can help you mitigate risks.

Collaborating with legal experts familiar with international IP laws is vital for safeguarding your creations. Ignoring these global issues can lead to costly disputes, lost revenue, and damage to your brand's reputation.

Handling IP disputes in the digital space

Steering through IP disputes in the digital domain can be intimidating, especially given the rapid pace of technological change and the fluidity of online interactions. You'll need to be proactive and informed to navigate potential conflicts effectively.

First, understanding the nature of the intellectual property at stake is essential. Are you dealing with copyrights, trademarks, or patents? Each type of IP has its own legal nuances and protections, so knowing what you own and how it's protected is your first line of defense.

Next, documentation is key. Maintain thorough records of your creations and their usage. This can include timestamps, drafts, and correspondence, which provide evidence of ownership and the timeline of your work.

When a dispute arises, this documentation can be invaluable in establishing your claims.

You should also be prepared to engage in negotiation or alternative dispute resolution methods. Litigation can be costly and time-consuming, particularly in the digital sphere, where jurisdictional issues can complicate matters. Mediation or arbitration might offer quicker, more amicable solutions.

Lastly, stay updated on the evolving laws and regulations surrounding IP in the digital landscape. The legal environment is fluid, and what applies today may change tomorrow.

IP implications for mobile and indie games

Mobile and indie games are often at the forefront of innovation, but with that creativity comes significant intellectual property (IP) implications. As a developer, you need to recognize how to protect your creations while navigating the complexities of IP law. Understanding these implications is essential for sustainable growth in this competitive market.

Consider these key points:

- **Copyrights**: Protect your original game design, code, and art.

- **Trademarks**: Register your game title and logo to secure your brand identity.

- **Patents**: Explore patent options for unique gameplay mechanics or technologies.

- **Licensing**: If using third-party assets, verify you comply with usage rights.

- **Fair Use**: Understand how this doctrine applies to your content, especially in fan-made games.

These elements are critical for safeguarding your work and avoiding infringement claims. The mobile and indie gaming landscape is rife with creativity, making it too easy for ideas to overlap.

Without proper IP management, you risk losing your competitive edge or facing legal battles that could derail your project.

Investing time in understanding IP rights protects your work and enhances your credibility as a developer. As you innovate, confirm that you're also building a robust IP strategy.

Case studies: IP infringement in gaming

Numerous case studies illustrate the complexities of IP infringement in gaming, highlighting the importance of understanding these legal boundaries.

Take the infamous case of Fortnite vs. PlayerUnknown's Battlegrounds (PUBG). Epic Games was accused of copying gameplay mechanics and features from PUBG. While Epic argued that many game elements were part of a broader genre, the dispute raised critical questions about originality and fair use in game design. This case emphasizes the thin line developers walk between inspiration and infringement.

Another notable example is *Zynga's* legal battle with *FarmVille*. The company faced claims from *Farm Town* creators for allegedly copying game mechanics and graphics. The outcome showcased how even highly successful companies must traverse the intricate web of IP laws as original creators endeavor to protect their innovations.

This case served as a cautionary tale, urging developers to guarantee their products reflect unique creativity rather than imitation.

Finally, consider the *Rockstar Games* vs. *Take-Two Interactive* scenario over using unauthorized mods. Rockstar's attempts to enforce IP rights against modders sparked debates about community creativity versus proprietary rights. This highlights the ongoing tension in gaming—where fan engagement can clash with IP protection.

These examples exemplify the necessity for game developers to understand IP laws deeply. Ignoring these legal frameworks can lead to costly litigation and reputational damage.

Ultimately, traversing IP in gaming requires a delicate balance between innovation and respect for existing rights.

Role of Digital Rights Management (DRM)

Digital rights management (DRM) is essential in safeguarding intellectual property in the gaming industry. It protects against piracy and ensures that creators receive the compensation they deserve for their work. Without effective DRM, developers risk losing significant revenue and motivation to innovate.

Here's why DRM is important:

- **Prevents Unauthorized Distribution**: DRM restricts the sharing of copyrighted content, limiting access to only those who've purchased the game.

- **Encourages Investment**: A secure environment makes publishers feel more confident about investing in new projects, knowing their intellectual property is protected.

- **Supports Fair Competition**: By leveling the playing field, DRM helps smaller developers compete against larger studios, fostering a healthier gaming ecosystem.

- **Enhances User Experience**: Many DRM solutions have user-friendly features, like cloud saves and automatic updates, improving overall gameplay.

- **Facilitates Legal Enforcement**: DRM facilitates the tracking and enforcement of copyright laws, making it simpler to address infringement cases.

However, it's important to strike a balance. Overly restrictive DRM can frustrate legitimate users and lead to backlash.

You'll want to evaluate how these systems can be implemented without alienating your audience. In the evolving landscape of gaming, understanding the nuanced role of DRM in protecting intellectual property isn't just beneficial; it's imperative for the industry's sustainability.

Embracing effective DRM strategies will empower you to safeguard your creations while providing players an enjoyable experience.

The future of IP law as it meets game design

As innovation propels the gaming industry forward, intellectual property (IP) law and game design intersection is becoming increasingly complex. As game mechanics evolve and new technologies emerge, IP law must adapt to protect the interests of creators without stifling creativity.

The challenge lies in balancing the rights of developers and the expectations of players, especially in an era where user-generated content is thriving.

Consider how the rise of mods and fan-made content shakes up traditional IP frameworks. These contributions can enhance a game's longevity but also pose infringement risks. You should recognize that adaptive licensing agreements could provide a solution, allowing developers to permit certain modifications while retaining control over their IP. This fosters community engagement and creates a revenue stream through official channels.

Moreover, the advent of blockchain technology introduces new possibilities for IP management. With smart contracts, you can guarantee that creators receive royalties whenever their work is used or sold. This technology could redefine ownership in gaming, making it more transparent and equitable.

As you navigate this evolving landscape, staying informed about emerging trends and legal interpretations is essential.

The future of IP law in gaming hinges on a collaborative approach that respects both innovation and legal protections. Embrace these changes, and you'll find opportunities to shape a fairer and more dynamic gaming environment that benefits everyone involved.

Chapter Four

Player Rights and Consumer Protection

As you navigate the complex landscape of the gaming industry, it's essential to understand your rights as a player and the protections available to you. With the rise of digital gaming, issues like data privacy, informed consent, and the risks associated with loot boxes have come to the forefront. How do these factors impact your gaming experience? And what legal frameworks are in place to guarantee a fair and secure environment? Exploring these questions reveals the intricate balance between enjoyment and protection that defines modern gaming.

Overview of player rights in gaming environments

As gaming continues to evolve, understanding your rights as a player in various gaming environments becomes increasingly critical. In today's digital landscape, players interact with various gaming platforms, each with rules and regulations.

It's crucial to recognize that your rights often vary depending on whether you're playing a single-player game, a multiplayer online environment, or a virtual reality experience.

One of your fundamental rights is the right to clear and transparent information about the game itself. Developers should provide accurate descriptions, including gameplay mechanics, pricing models, and in-game purchases. Misleading information can lead to frustration and a sense of betrayal among players.

You also have the right to a safe gaming environment. This encompasses not just the technical aspects—like the protection of personal data and the prevention of harassment—but also the assurance that the game won't expose you to harmful content without proper warnings.

Developers should enforce community standards that foster respectful interactions.

Additionally, you possess the right to seek redress if you encounter issues like bugs, server outages, or unfair practices. Many platforms offer support channels where you can voice your concerns, and reputable developers will endeavor to address your grievances.

Ultimately, being informed about your rights empowers you as a player. It enhances your gaming experience and encourages developers to maintain higher standards, ensuring a fair and enjoyable environment for everyone involved.

Consumer protection laws in gaming and gambling

What do consumer protection laws mean for players in the gaming and gambling industries? These laws serve as a safety net, guaranteeing that your rights as a player are upheld. They regulate gaming companies' operations, aiming to create a fair and transparent environment. You can expect accurate information about games, fair odds, and reliable payout processes.

One significant aspect of consumer protection laws is the requirement for transparency. Gaming companies must disclose the odds of winning in gambling games and provide clear terms of service. This transparency allows you to make informed decisions about your participation.

Additionally, regulations often mandate that companies implement responsible gaming measures, such as self-exclusion options and betting limits, designed to protect vulnerable players from excessive gambling.

Furthermore, consumer protection laws tackle issues related to fraud and scams. If a gaming company fails to deliver its promised services or engages in deceptive practices, these laws give you recourse. You can file complaints with regulatory bodies, which can investigate and take action against violators.

Finally, these laws guarantee that your personal information is safeguarded. Gaming companies are typically required to implement robust security measures to protect your data from breaches. This helps maintain your privacy and builds trust in the gaming environment.

Consumer protection laws play an essential role in shaping a safer, fairer gaming landscape, giving you confidence in your gaming and gambling experiences.

Informed consent in gaming terms and conditions

Understanding the importance of informed consent in gaming terms and conditions is crucial for players maneuvering the complex landscape of online gaming. When you sign up for a game or platform, you're often required to accept terms and conditions that can be lengthy and filled with legal jargon. This process should guarantee that you fully understand your rights, obligations, and potential risks involved in the gaming experience.

Informed consent means that you know what you're agreeing to and make decisions based on clear, accessible information. Unfortunately, many players skim through these extensive documents, missing critical details about gameplay, payment structures, and the implications of their data usage. This lack of understanding could lead to unintended consequences, such as hidden fees or restrictive clauses that limit your rights as a player.

To enhance your informed consent, developers should endeavor to present terms and conditions in a user-friendly manner. This includes summarizing key points and using plain language to explain complex legal terms.

As a player, you should actively seek to understand these documents, asking questions or seeking clarification when needed. Doing so empowers you to make informed decisions about the games you play and the platforms you choose.

Ultimately, informed consent isn't just a legal formality; it's a fundamental aspect of guaranteeing your rights in the gaming industry. Comprehending terms and conditions can considerably impact your overall gaming experience.

Data protection and privacy for players

Data protection and privacy are paramount for players traversing the digital landscape of gaming. As you engage with various platforms, your data is often collected, stored, and used in ways that mightn't be immediately apparent. Understanding your rights regarding this data is fundamental for safeguarding your personal information.

Here are three essential aspects of data protection and privacy that every player should consider:

1. **Informed Consent**: Before sharing personal information, ensure you know how your data will be used. Game developers should provide clear, concise privacy policies outlining data collection practices.

2. **Data Security**: It is critical to choose gaming platforms that prioritize data security. Look for features like encryption and secure servers to protect your data from unauthorized access. A reputable company will invest in robust security measures to protect your information.

3. **Your Right to Access and Control**: You can access the data collected about you and request its deletion. Familiarize yourself with the procedures for obtaining your data and how to exercise your rights. This empowers you to maintain control over your personal information.

In today's gaming environment, being proactive about data protection and privacy isn't just wise; it's indispensable. By staying informed and vigilant, you can navigate gaming while protecting your personal information effectively.

Age restrictions and minor protection

Age restrictions play an important role in protecting minors in the gaming industry. These regulations guarantee that young players are shielded from content that may be inappropriate or harmful. By establishing age ratings, such as those from the Entertainment Software Rating Board (ESRB) or

Pan European Game Information (PEGI), the industry provides guidance to consumers. You can easily identify which games are suitable based on the age recommendations.

However, it's important to recognize that these systems rely on accurate enforcement. Parents and guardians must be vigilant, as they often play a significant role in monitoring their children's gaming activities. You should educate yourself about the various ratings and what they signify. For instance, a game rated "M for Mature" may contain intense violence, explicit content, or strong language—elements inappropriate for younger audiences.

Moreover, game developers and publishers are responsible for adhering to these age restrictions. They must clearly display ratings on packaging and digital storefronts, ensuring players know what they purchase. This transparency is essential not only for consumer protection but also for fostering a responsible gaming culture.

Lastly, age restrictions are a solid foundation, but they aren't foolproof. As technology evolves, so do the ways minors can access games. You should advocate for better tools and parental controls that empower guardians to manage gaming access effectively. By staying informed and proactive, you can help protect minors from unsuitable content in the gaming landscape.

Addressing addiction and mental health issues

While age restrictions help safeguard minors from inappropriate content, they don't address the growing concern of addiction and mental health issues associated with gaming.

As you immerse yourself in the digital world, it's vital to recognize how excessive gaming can impact your mental health. The gaming industry must take responsibility for addressing these concerns by implementing effective measures.

Here are three strategies that can help mitigate addiction and promote mental well-being:

1. **Implementing Time Limits**: Developers can incorporate in-game features that allow players to set time limits on their gaming sessions. This encourages balanced gameplay and helps prevent excessive hours spent in front of a screen.

2. **Promoting Mental Health Resources**: Game publishers should create awareness about mental health resources within their games. Including links to support hotlines or providing educational content about gaming addiction can empower players to seek help when needed.

3. **Encouraging Community Support**: Fostering a supportive gaming community is essential. Developers can integrate forums or social features that encourage players to share experiences and strategies for maintaining a healthy relationship with gaming.

Fairness in gameplay and transparency

Fairness in gameplay and transparency are fundamental for maintaining player trust and engagement in the gaming industry. When you participate in games, you expect an environment where skill and effort determine success, not hidden algorithms or biased mechanics. Developers must guarantee that all players have equal opportunities, adhering to standards that promote integrity and competitiveness.

If you feel the outcome is manipulated or unjust, your enthusiasm for the game diminishes, leading to disengagement.

Transparency plays an important role in this situation. You deserve to know how games operate, including the mechanics behind loot boxes, in-game purchases, and matchmaking systems. Clear communication about odds and probabilities empowers you to make informed decisions. When developers disclose this information, they comply with regulations and foster a sense of loyalty among players.

Moreover, fairness extends to player treatment. You should have access to clear rules and guidelines that dictate gameplay. This guarantees everyone is on the same page and reduces ambiguity regarding disputes and penalties.

Developers must swiftly implement systems that recognize and address grievances, demonstrating a fairness commitment.

Refunds, returns, and consumer complaints

Steering through the complexities of refunds, returns, and consumer complaints is fundamental for players in the gaming industry. Understanding your rights can help you navigate potential pitfalls and guarantee you're treated fairly. Many players often overlook the significant processes that govern how and when they can seek refunds or returns for their purchases.

Here are three key points to take into account:

1. **Know the Policy**: Each game publisher or platform usually has a refund policy. Familiarizing yourself with these terms can save you headaches later. Policies often specify time limits for requesting refunds and the conditions for accepting returns.

2. **Document Everything**: When you encounter an issue, keeping

records of your transactions and any communications with customer support is essential. This documentation will be fundamental if you must escalate your complaint or provide evidence for a refund claim.

3. **Utilize Support Channels**: Most gaming platforms offer multiple ways to resolve consumer complaints, including chat support, email, or forums. Engaging through the appropriate channels can lead to quicker resolutions. Be polite and precise when explaining your issue to guarantee a smooth process.

Player recourse in case of disputes

Knowing your options can make all the difference when disputes arise in the gaming industry. You may find yourself in a situation where a game doesn't function as advertised, or perhaps you believe you've been unfairly banned from a platform. Understanding your recourse is essential to protecting your rights as a player.

First, you should always start with the customer support channels offered by the game or platform. Most gaming companies provide help desks, chat support, or email services that can address your concerns directly. Clearly outline your issue and provide relevant documentation, such as receipts or screenshots, to strengthen your case.

If direct support doesn't yield satisfactory results, consider escalating the matter. Many companies have formal complaint processes or ombudsmen that handle unresolved issues. Document all your communications to create a solid record of your attempts to resolve the dispute.

Should those efforts fall short, you might explore alternative dispute resolution (ADR) methods, like mediation or arbitration. These methods can often be quicker and less costly than traditional litigation, and they may be required under the terms of service you accepted when joining the platform.

Legal protections against harassment and abuse

Understanding your rights in disputes is just the beginning; players also have legal protections against harassment and abuse within the gaming community. These protections are essential for creating a safe environment to enjoy gaming without fear of mistreatment. Various laws and policies aim to safeguard players, ensuring that harassment and abuse are addressed effectively.

Here are three key legal protections you should be aware of:

1. **Anti-Harassment Laws**: Many jurisdictions have anti-harassment laws that extend to online interactions. These laws can provide recourse if you're subjected to threats, hate speech, or targeted harassment based on protected characteristics such as race, gender, or sexual orientation.

2. **Terms of Service Violations**: Gaming companies often include specific policies regarding acceptable behavior in their Terms of Service. If another player violates these terms, you can report them to the company. Many platforms take such reports seriously, leading to potential bans or penalties for the offending party.

3. **Reporting Mechanisms**: Most gaming platforms offer robust reporting mechanisms that allow players to flag abusive behavior. By utilizing these tools, you protect yourself and contribute to a healthier gaming community.

Understanding these protections empowers you to advocate for your rights and seek recourse when needed. Remember, you're not alone; there are legal avenues available to help you combat harassment and abuse in the gaming world.

Importance of clear labeling in in-game purchases

Clear labeling in in-game purchases is essential for players to make informed decisions about their spending. You often encounter various purchasing options when you engage with a game, from cosmetic items to gameplay enhancements. Without clear labels, it's easy to misinterpret the value and implications of these purchases. You deserve transparency in your buying and how it affects your gaming experience.

Clear labeling helps you differentiate between one-time purchases, subscriptions, and recurring payments. You can budget accordingly when a game clearly states that a purchase is a one-off. Conversely, if a label indicates a subscription, you can assess whether the ongoing cost fits your financial plans. This clarity minimizes the risk of unexpected charges if you inadvertently sign up for something you didn't fully understand.

Moreover, precise labeling fosters trust between game developers and players. You're more likely to feel confident in your decisions when you see clear, honest communication regarding in-game purchases. This trust is vital, especially in an industry where microtransactions and loot boxes have raised concerns about exploitation.

Risks of loot boxes and microtransactions

Traversing the landscape of loot boxes and microtransactions presents significant risks for players, often leading to unexpected financial burdens.

While these features can enhance gameplay, they can also create a cycle of dependency and overspending. Understanding these risks is essential for protecting your rights as a consumer.

1. **Financial Overreach**: Getting caught up in the excitement of a loot box or microtransaction is easy. You might think spending just a few dollars here and there won't add up, but those small amounts can quickly escalate, leading you to spend far more than intended.

2. **Gambling-like Mechanics**: Many loot boxes employ a random reward system that mimics gambling. You might find yourself chasing that rare item, which can lead to compulsive spending habits.

The thrill of chance can overshadow rational decision-making, risking your financial well-being.

3. **Lack of Transparency**: Often, the odds of obtaining desirable items in loot boxes aren't disclosed. This lack of transparency can mislead you into believing you have a better chance of winning than you actually do.

The uncertainty surrounding these purchases can lead to frustration and disappointment, fueling the urge to spend more.

Laws on deceptive practices in advertising

The financial risks associated with loot boxes and microtransactions often intersect with laws addressing deceptive practices in advertising. In the gaming industry, misleading marketing can entice players into spending money on in-game purchases without fully understanding what they're getting. This is where consumer protection laws, particularly those designed to combat false advertising, come into play.

You should be aware that the Federal Trade Commission (FTC) enforces regulations requiring advertising to be truthful and not misleading. If a game falsely represents the odds of winning a valuable item in a loot box, it might violate these laws. Similarly, if an advertisement implies that a player will achieve certain outcomes without clarifying the randomness involved, it could be deemed deceptive.

Many countries have begun to scrutinize these practices more closely. For instance, the U.K. has taken steps to regulate loot boxes under gambling laws, suggesting that misleading advertising could lead to legal repercussions. Additionally, transparency in advertising is essential. Game developers must clearly disclose what players can expect when they purchase loot boxes or microtransactions.

As a player, you have the right to demand honesty in advertising. You can file complaints with consumer protection agencies if a game's promotional materials mislead you. Understanding these laws empowers you as a consumer and holds the gaming industry accountable for its marketing practices.

Fraud prevention and anti-cheat measures

In recent years, the gaming industry has faced increasing scrutiny regarding fraud prevention and anti-cheat measures, with nearly 80% of players expressing concern over cheating in online games.

This concern underscores the necessity for robust strategies that guarantee fair play and protect player rights. You, as a player, deserve a gaming environment where your efforts are rewarded without the interference of dishonest practices.

To effectively combat fraud and cheating, game developers are implementing several measures:

1. **Advanced Detection Systems**: Many companies invest in sophisticated algorithms that analyze player behavior, identifying patterns that indicate cheating, such as unusual score progressions

or unauthorized modifications.

2. **Regular Updates and Patches**: Frequent updates improve gameplay and help close vulnerabilities that cheaters exploit. These patches guarantee that the game remains challenging and fair for all players.

3. **Community Reporting Tools**: Empowering players to report suspicious behavior fosters a community-driven approach to maintaining integrity. When you can easily report potential cheaters, developers gain valuable insights that help enforce rules more effectively.

Ensuring accessibility for all users

As the gaming industry prioritizes fair play through anti-cheat measures, it also faces the challenge of guaranteeing accessibility for all users. Accessibility isn't just a legal obligation; it's a moral imperative that enhances the gaming experience for everyone.

With a diverse player base, developers must consider various disabilities and needs, from visual impairments to motor skill challenges. To achieve true inclusivity, you should advocate for universal design principles. This involves creating games that cater to a wide range of abilities.

For instance, implementing customizable controls allows players to tailor gameplay to their needs. Closed captioning and audio descriptions can greatly enhance the experience for those with hearing or visual impairments.

Moreover, you need to support initiatives that promote awareness and training within the industry. Developers should engage with accessibility consultants and disabled gamers during the design process to identify potential barriers. Regular testing with diverse user groups can help guarantee that games are genuinely accessible before launch.

Additionally, consider the role of regulatory frameworks. Governments and gaming organizations can incentivize developers to prioritize accessibility through grants or awards. You should encourage transparency, urging companies to publish accessibility features and updates, allowing players to make informed decisions.

Chapter Five

Monetization Models and Legal Ramifications

In today's gaming landscape, you're likely encountering a variety of monetization models, each with its own set of legal challenges. Understanding the legal implications becomes essential as you explore premium sales, freemium structures, or subscription services. From consumer protection laws to the nuances of in-app purchases, the potential for unforeseen complications looms large. Additionally, as microtransactions grow in popularity, you might question the ethical boundaries of these practices. What happens when a model crosses the line, and how does it impact your bottom line?

Examining different monetization models

Understanding various monetization models is essential for developers and players alike in today's gaming landscape. You'll encounter several key models that shape the way games generate revenue. The most common include premium sales, freemium, subscription services, and advertising.

Premium sales are straightforward; you pay upfront for a game. This model provides a complete experience without additional costs, appealing to players who prefer a one-time investment. However, it limits developers' potential for ongoing revenue.

Freemium models allow players to download and play a game for free, with optional in-game purchases. This approach has gained popularity as it attracts a larger audience. You can enjoy the core game without spending, but developers monetize through microtransactions for cosmetic items, boosts, or additional content.

While this model can maximize revenue, it raises concerns about balancing gameplay and monetization.

Subscription services, like Xbox Game Pass or Apple Arcade, provide access to a library of games for a monthly fee. This model guarantees a steady revenue stream for developers and offers players a vast selection without individual purchases.

It fosters a community-centric approach, encouraging engagement but potentially fragmenting player bases.

Advertising, particularly in mobile games, serves as another monetization avenue. You'll often see ads integrated into gameplay or offered as optional viewing for rewards.

While this can be lucrative, it risks disrupting the player experience.

Legal considerations for in-app purchases

Developers must navigate a complex landscape of legal regulations and guidelines when contemplating in-app purchases. The first step is understanding consumer protection laws, which often require transparency regarding the costs associated with in-app purchases. You need to guarantee that users are fully informed before they engage in transactions. This includes clear labeling of items and services and making it obvious when users are about to incur charges.

Moreover, payment processing regulations play a significant role in structuring in-app purchases. Many jurisdictions mandate that developers use specific payment systems, particularly for digital goods. Failure to comply can lead to hefty fines or removal from app stores.

It's also essential to consider age restrictions; implementing age verification mechanisms can mitigate the legal risks associated with minors making unauthorized purchases.

Another critical aspect is data protection. You must secure users' financial information and comply with regulations like the General Data Protection Regulation (GDPR). Non-compliance can result in significant penalties and damage to your reputation.

Additionally, consider the implications of subscription-based models, which often have their own legal considerations. While this may be a topic for later discussion, being aware of these dynamics now can inform your approach to in-app purchases.

Subscription models and contractual obligations

Subscription models have become increasingly popular in the gaming industry, offering developers a steady revenue stream while fostering ongoing relationships with players. These models typically involve players paying a recurring fee in exchange for access to content, features, or services. However, this arrangement also brings about complex contractual obligations that both parties must understand to mitigate legal risks.

When you subscribe to a game, you enter into a contract, often governed by terms of service. These terms outline your rights and obligations, including payment schedules, cancellation policies, and limitations on usage. You need to read these agreements carefully, as they can contain clauses that limit your ability to seek legal recourse in case of disputes.

From the developer's perspective, subscription models necessitate transparent communication regarding changes in pricing, content availability, and service quality. Players expect regular updates and value for their money, which can lead to reputational risks if not managed properly.

Additionally, developers must guarantee compliance with consumer protection laws, which may vary by jurisdiction. This includes addressing issues like automatic renewals, which some jurisdictions require explicit consent.

In essence, subscription models create a framework of mutual obligations where both parties must know their rights. Understanding these contractual dynamics allows you to navigate the gaming landscape more effectively, ensuring you enjoy your gaming experience while safeguarding your legal interests.

Understanding "freemium" and free-to-play models

As the gaming industry evolves, monetization strategies like freemium and free-to-play models have gained traction alongside subscription options. These models allow you to access games without an upfront cost, making them appealing to a broad audience.

However, they also raise significant questions about consumer behavior and ethical practices.

Freemium models often provide a base game for free but encourage players to purchase additional content or features. In contrast, free-to-play games are entirely free but may include microtransactions for in-game items or advantages. Understanding these concepts is fundamental for maneuvering the gaming landscape effectively.

Here are some key points to reflect on regarding these models:

- **User Acquisition**: Freemium and free-to-play models attract a larger player base, often leading to higher engagement.

- **Revenue Generation**: Monetization occurs through microtransactions, sometimes leading to player frustration if not handled transparently.

- **Gameplay Balance**: Developers must guarantee that spending doesn't create an unfair advantage, sustaining enjoyment for all players.

- **Consumer Perception**: Players may view these models skeptically, worrying about "pay-to-win" dynamics.

- **Regulatory Scrutiny**: As these models become more common, they may attract regulatory attention regarding ethical marketing and consumer protection.

Regulating microtransactions and virtual goods

Regulating microtransactions and virtual goods has become a pressing concern in the gaming industry, particularly as these practices expand rapidly. As you delve into this domain, it's critical to recognize the complexities surrounding player spending habits and the ethical implications of monetization strategies.

Many gamers find microtransactions frustrating, especially when these purchases impact gameplay or create a pay-to-win environment. Governments and regulatory bodies are increasingly scrutinizing these models to protect consumers, especially minors, who may not fully understand the financial implications of in-game purchases.

The lack of transparency in how these transactions work often leads to questions about fairness and consumer rights. You'll notice that some jurisdictions have already begun implementing regulations requiring game developers to disclose the odds of obtaining specific items through microtransactions, much like gambling laws.

Data privacy concerns arise from collecting user information associated with these transactions. As you navigate this landscape, it's important to reflect on how regulations can guarantee that personal data is handled responsibly and that users are informed about their rights.

Ultimately, striking a balance between fostering innovation and protecting consumers is essential. Developers must adapt to these regulations while remaining competitive in a rapidly evolving market.

Understanding the legal ramifications surrounding microtransactions and virtual goods will not only help you comply but also help you design fairer gaming experiences that respect player investment and enhance overall enjoyment.

Compliance for eSports betting and fantasy sports

The rise of eSports betting and fantasy sports has introduced new layers of complexity regarding compliance and regulation within the gaming industry. As these sectors grow, understanding the legal requirements becomes essential for operators, players, and regulators.

Compliance guarantees that you navigate the evolving landscape while mitigating risks associated with legal repercussions.

Here are some critical aspects of compliance in eSports betting and fantasy sports:

- **Licensing Requirements**: Operators must secure the proper licenses in their jurisdictions to legally offer betting services.

- **Age Verification**: Strict age verification processes are necessary to guarantee that only legal-age individuals participate in betting and fantasy sports.

- **Consumer Protections**: Regulations often mandate transparency in odds, payout structures, and the handling of customer funds to protect players from fraud.

- **Responsible Gaming Measures**: Operators must implement policies to promote responsible gambling, including self-exclusion options and limits on betting amounts.

- **Data Privacy Regulations**: Compliance with data protection laws, such as the GDPR, is essential, particularly when handling personal information from players.

Tax implications in gaming revenue models

Understanding the tax implications of gaming revenue models is essential for operators seeking to maximize profitability while remaining compliant with legal obligations. Depending on jurisdiction, different revenue models—like in-game purchases, subscriptions, and ad revenues—can trigger varied tax liabilities. For instance, sales tax may apply to digital goods, whereas income tax will affect the revenues generated.

Operators must also consider the nature of their revenue streams. If you're running a gambling platform, the taxation can become particularly complex. Many jurisdictions impose specific gaming taxes that can substantially impact your bottom line. These taxes often depend on the type of gaming offered, such as sports betting or casino-style games, and can range from flat rates to percentages of revenue.

Additionally, cross-border issues arise when dealing with international players. Understanding where your players are located can influence how you approach tax compliance. You might face withholding taxes on winnings and requirements to report and remit taxes to various jurisdictions, complicating your accounting processes.

Maintain meticulous records of all financial transactions, as tax authorities may demand transparency. Failure to comply with tax obligations can lead to severe penalties, including fines and potential legal action.

Consequently, seeking advice from tax professionals with experience in the gaming industry can help you navigate these complexities effectively, ensuring your operations remain profitable and compliant.

Distinguishing gambling vs. monetized gaming

Tax implications are just one piece of the puzzle regarding gaming revenue generation. Understanding the distinction between gambling and monetized gaming is essential for maneuvering through legal frameworks.

While both involve financial transactions, their core mechanics and intent differ greatly.

In gambling, players wager real money on uncertain outcomes, often with the possibility of losing their stake. Conversely, monetized gaming typically focuses on enhancing the gaming experience through optional purchases or in-game currencies without the primary goal of financial gain. Here's how you can differentiate them:

- **Wagering**: Gambling involves placing bets on games of chance; monetized gaming usually offers purchases that enhance gameplay but don't require a monetary stake.

- **Outcomes**: In gambling, outcomes are uncertain and primarily depend on chance; monetized gaming often relies on player skill or strategy.

- **Return on Investment**: Gambling can yield real monetary returns; monetized gaming may provide in-game benefits but doesn't guarantee financial rewards.

- **Regulatory Oversight**: Gambling is heavily regulated in most jurisdictions, while monetized gaming often falls under consumer protection laws instead.

- **Player Intent**: Gamblers seek financial profit; players in monetized gaming aim for enjoyment and improved experiences.

Understanding virtual currencies in gaming

Exploring the territory of virtual currencies in gaming reveals a complex ecosystem that enhances player engagement and monetization strategies. Virtual currencies, often represented as in-game tokens or credits, allow players to purchase items, access content, or enhance gameplay experiences. These currencies can be earned through gameplay or purchased with real money, creating a dual-layered economy that benefits players and developers.

You'll notice that virtual currencies foster a sense of progression and achievement. Developers encourage continued engagement and investment by providing players with a mechanism to accumulate wealth within the game. This system also allows for diverse monetization opportunities, as players may feel incentivized to spend real money to expedite their in-game progress.

However, implementing virtual currencies isn't without challenges. Developers must navigate a landscape of consumer expectations and legal regulations. Issues arise regarding the transparency of currency acquisition methods and the potential for players to feel exploited by aggressive monetization tactics.

Furthermore, maintaining a balanced economy is imperative; if virtual currencies become too easily obtained, their value may diminish, undermining the intended player experience.

As you investigate this domain further, it's important to recognize the legal implications surrounding virtual currencies. Regulatory bodies are increasingly scrutinizing how these currencies function within games, particularly concerning consumer protection and fair trading practices.

Understanding these dynamics is fundamental for developers aiming to create sustainable and legally compliant monetization strategies in the gaming industry.

Loot boxes, laws, and ethical questions

Loot boxes have stirred up significant debate in the gaming community, raising pressing legal and ethical questions. You might wonder about their implications as you engage with games that feature these monetization strategies.

These digital containers offer randomized rewards, but they also blur the lines between gaming and gambling, causing concern among regulators and players alike.

Consider the following ethical and legal concerns surrounding loot boxes:

- **Gambling Risk**: The behavior of purchasing loot boxes mirrors gambling, particularly for younger audiences.

- **Transparency**: Many games lack clear information on the odds of receiving specific items, leading to accusations of deceptive practices.

- **Consumer Protection**: Laws regarding consumer rights may not adequately cover digital goods, raising questions about refunds and disputes.

- **Mental Health**: The potential for addiction and its impact on mental health is a significant concern, especially for vulnerable players.

- **Regulatory Response**: Different countries are approaching loot boxes with varying laws, complicating compliance for game developers.

As you navigate the complex landscape of loot boxes, you must remain informed about the evolving legal frameworks.

The balance between monetization innovation and ethical responsibility is delicate. Developers must consider their audience and the potential consequences of incorporating loot boxes into their games while recognizing the broader implications for the gaming industry.

Gaming laws and crypto payments

As the gaming industry continues to evolve, the integration of cryptocurrency payments is becoming a significant talking point, especially in light of ongoing discussions around monetization strategies like loot boxes. The rise of blockchain technology offers a new layer of complexity to gaming laws, necessitating a careful examination of how these digital currencies interact with existing regulations.

The legal landscape surrounding crypto payments in gaming is multifaceted. Different jurisdictions treat cryptocurrencies differently, ranging from outright bans to full acceptance. For instance, some countries may classify cryptocurrencies as currency, while others consider them securities. This classification affects how games can implement crypto payments and what legal obligations they must meet.

One major concern is consumer protection. With the anonymity that cryptocurrencies offer, players might face increased risks of fraud or exploitation. Gamers should pay close attention to the regulations in their respective regions, as developers are often required to implement measures that protect players from potential abuses linked to crypto transactions.

Additionally, compliance with anti-money laundering (AML) and know your customer (KYC) regulations is vital. Game developers might need to establish protocols to verify the identities of players engaging in crypto transactions, guaranteeing that they adhere to legal standards.

Ultimately, as you navigate the evolving landscape of gaming laws and cryptocurrency payments, staying informed about regulatory trends will guarantee compliance and player safety in this dynamic environment.

Taxation on winnings in gambling platforms

Many players are often surprised to learn about the tax implications of their winnings on gambling platforms. It's vital to recognize that gambling winnings are generally considered taxable income in many jurisdictions, and the responsibility for reporting these winnings falls squarely on you. The rules can vary markedly depending on where you live, so understanding the specifics is important.

Here are some key points to reflect on regarding taxation on your gambling winnings:

- **Income Reporting**: You must report all winnings on your annual tax return regardless of the amount.

- **Tax Rates**: The tax rate applied to your winnings may depend on your total income bracket.

- **Deductible Losses**: You can often deduct gambling losses, but only if you itemize your deductions.

- **Documentation**: Keep accurate records of your wins and losses; this documentation is crucial for substantiating your claims.

- **State vs. Federal Obligations**: Be aware that federal and state taxes may apply, with state laws varying widely.

Failure to report your gambling income can lead to penalties and interest charges. Some platforms may also withhold taxes on large winnings, but this doesn't relieve you of the responsibility to report all income.

Always consult with a tax professional familiar with gambling laws in your jurisdiction to guarantee compliance and optimize your tax situation.

Understanding these implications will help you navigate your winnings more effectively and avoid potential legal repercussions.

Case studies: Legal consequences of model changes

Changes in monetization models within the gaming industry can lead to significant legal consequences, particularly when players navigate the complexities of new regulations. For instance, consider the shift from a one-time purchase model to a free-to-play model with microtransactions. When this alteration occurred, some developers faced lawsuits over deceptive practices, as players felt misled about the actual costs associated with in-game purchases. This litigation highlights the need for transparency in pricing and consumer protection.

Another notable case is the introduction of loot boxes, which some jurisdictions have classified as gambling due to their randomized rewards. This classification prompted legal challenges in various countries, resulting in legislation aimed at regulating or outright banning loot boxes. As a player, you might find that the legal landscape surrounding loot boxes affects your gaming experience and potential repercussions for developers who fail to comply.

Moreover, a change in advertising practices can also yield legal ramifications. When a popular game switched to aggressive ad placements, it faced backlash from users and regulatory scrutiny for violating advertising standards. This scenario underscores the importance of understanding consumer rights and the legal framework governing game advertising.

International laws affecting global monetization

Maneuvering the complex landscape of international laws is essential for developers aiming to monetize their games globally. Each country has regulations that can greatly impact how you implement monetization strategies. Understanding these laws is imperative to avoid legal pitfalls and guarantee compliance while maximizing revenue potential.

Here are some key international legal considerations you should keep in mind:

- **Consumer Protection Laws**: Different jurisdictions enforce regulations that protect consumers from unfair practices, affecting how you advertise and price your in-game purchases.

- **Data Privacy Regulations**: Laws like GDPR in Europe mandate strict guidelines on how you collect, store, and use player data, impacting your marketing and monetization strategies.

- **Intellectual Property Rights**: These laws vary widely, influencing how you can use existing IP within your games and how you protect your own creations.

- **Taxation Policies**: Different countries have varying tax obligations on digital sales, affecting your bottom line and pricing strategies.

- **Gambling Regulations**: If your game includes mechanics resembling gambling, you must navigate the legal landscape surrounding gaming laws in different territories.

As you explore global markets, staying informed about these laws will allow you to develop monetization strategies that aren't only profitable and legally compliant.

Ignoring these regulations can lead to costly penalties and damage to your reputation, so it's essential to integrate legal considerations into your business model from the outset.

Forecast: Evolving models and future legalities

As the gaming industry evolves, developers must anticipate shifts in monetization models and the legal frameworks that govern them. The rise of subscription services and cloud gaming platforms indicates a significant change from traditional one-time purchase models. This shift will likely require developers to reassess revenue-sharing agreements and intellectual property protections, particularly as game content becomes more fluid and interdependent.

Furthermore, the growing concern over in-game purchases, especially those involving randomized loot boxes, has prompted regulatory scrutiny worldwide. You should prepare for potential legislation imposing stricter guidelines on how these monetization strategies are employed. Countries may impose age restrictions or require disclosures regarding odds, directly impacting your game design and marketing strategies.

Moreover, integrating blockchain technology and NFTs in gaming presents opportunities and challenges. While these technologies can create new revenue streams, you'll need to navigate the complex legal landscape surrounding digital ownership and copyright. As the market matures, regulatory bodies may establish clearer frameworks, but uncertainty will reign until then.

Lastly, consider the implications of data privacy regulations, such as the GDPR in Europe, which could affect how you collect and monetize user data. Adapting to these evolving models and legal landscapes will be essential in ensuring compliance while maximizing profitability.

Chapter Six

The Impact of Technology on Gaming Law

As you navigate the evolving landscape of gaming, it's clear that technology's rapid advancement is reshaping the legal framework surrounding the industry. New challenges arise with each innovation, from blockchain and NFTs to AI-driven moderation. You might wonder how these developments affect data privacy and consumer protection, especially as games become more immersive and interconnected. Understanding the implications of these changes is essential, and it raises important questions about the future of gaming law. What might the next wave of regulations look like, and how can you prepare for them?

Legal challenges introduced by new technology

The rapid evolution of technology in the gaming industry has sparked many legal challenges, fundamentally altering the landscape of gaming law. As you explore this dynamic domain, you'll notice that issues like data privacy, intellectual property rights, and consumer protection are at the forefront.

The rise of online gaming and cloud-based platforms has complicated how personal data is collected and used, raising significant concerns about user consent and the security of sensitive information. As regulations vary widely across jurisdictions, it might be vital to navigate these legal waters carefully.

Moreover, the advent of multiplayer and cross-platform gaming introduces additional copyright and trademark enforcement challenges. As players create and share content, the lines between fair use and infringement often blur.

You'll need to reflect on how these developments impact the ownership of in-game assets, particularly when user-generated content becomes commercially viable.

Furthermore, the increasing prevalence of microtransactions and loot boxes has drawn scrutiny from regulators concerned about gambling-like mechanics. As you assess these issues, understanding the implications of consumer protection laws will be essential to guarantee compliance and mitigate risks.

Staying informed about the evolving legal landscape is imperative in this rapidly changing environment. Engaging with legal experts and industry stakeholders can provide valuable insights that will equip you to tackle the unique challenges posed by new technologies in the gaming sector.

As technology advances, so will the legal frameworks that govern your gaming experience.

Blockchain, NFTs, and digital asset ownership

Many gaming enthusiasts are now exploring the intersection of blockchain technology, non-fungible tokens (NFTs), and digital asset ownership, reshaping how players interact with in-game items.

Blockchain offers a decentralized ledger that provides transparency and security, ensuring that ownership of digital assets is verifiable and immutable. This fundamentally changes how you perceive your in-game items, transforming them from mere pixels into real assets with tangible value.

NFTs serve as unique identifiers for these digital assets, allowing you to buy, sell, or trade them on various platforms. Unlike traditional in-game items, which are often locked within a specific game ecosystem, NFTs can be transferred across different games and platforms. This portability enhances your ability to build a collection and invest in assets you may appreciate.

However, the rise of blockchain and NFTs introduces legal complexities. You might wonder about the implications of ownership and intellectual property rights. While NFTs grant you ownership of a digital asset, the underlying rights to the content may still belong to the original creator or publisher.

This ambiguity can lead to disputes, particularly regarding copyright and licensing. As regulations evolve, you must stay informed about the legal landscape surrounding blockchain and NFTs.

Understanding how these technologies affect your rights and responsibilities will be essential in maneuvering this new frontier in gaming. Ultimately, embracing blockchain and NFTs can empower you as a player, but it also requires a keen awareness of the legal implications.

Artificial intelligence in gaming and regulation

As blockchain and NFTs redefine asset ownership within gaming, artificial intelligence (AI) is becoming increasingly significant in shaping player experiences and game mechanics. Developers harness AI to create dynamic gameplay, personalized experiences, and responsive in-game environments.

However, with these advancements comes the need for regulatory frameworks that guarantee fairness and transparency.

You might wonder how AI impacts gaming regulation. Here are three important considerations:

1. **Fairness**: AI can create algorithms that adjust difficulty levels based on player skill. Not properly regulated could lead to accusations of bias or unfair advantage.

2. **Data Privacy**: AI systems often collect and analyze player data to enhance experiences. Without strict regulations, there's a risk of misuse, leading to potential breaches of privacy laws.

3. **Content Creation**: AI-generated game content raises questions about copyright ownership and intellectual property. Who owns the rights to an AI-created character or story? This ambiguity can lead to legal disputes.

As the gaming industry embraces AI, it's essential to establish regulations that protect players while fostering innovation.

To navigate potential pitfalls, you'll need to stay informed about the evolving legal landscape surrounding AI. The balance between technological advancement and regulatory oversight is delicate but necessary for a fair and enjoyable gaming experience.

The future of gaming hinges not just on creativity but also on the laws that govern its evolution.

Augmented and virtual reality law implications

With the rise of augmented reality (AR) and virtual reality (VR) technologies, legal implications are becoming increasingly complex. As you navigate this evolving landscape, you'll find that issues surrounding intellectual property, user privacy, and liability take center stage.

First, consider intellectual property rights. AR and VR often incorporate existing copyrighted materials, such as digital representations of famous landmarks or characters from popular franchises. This raises questions about licensing agreements and the potential for copyright infringement.

You'll need to guarantee that any content you create respects these rights while understanding the legal nuances of transformative use.

Next, user privacy is a critical concern. AR and VR collect vast amounts of data, including personal information and behavioral patterns. This data can lead to significant privacy risks, especially if mishandled.

As a developer or user, you should stay informed about regulations like the General Data Protection Regulation (GDPR) and how they apply to data collected in immersive environments.

Lastly, liability issues arise when users experience accidents or injuries while using AR and VR technologies. Determining who's responsible—developers, hardware manufacturers, or even users—can be tricky.

You should know the legal precedents shaping liability in immersive experiences.

Navigating these legal implications requires a proactive approach. By staying informed and compliant, you can mitigate risks while leveraging AR and VR's innovative potential in gaming.

Cloud gaming: regulatory concerns

Cloud gaming is reshaping the landscape of video game consumption, but it also brings a host of regulatory concerns that require careful consideration. As you explore this evolving field, you'll quickly realize that the implications extend beyond mere gameplay.

Here are three key regulatory concerns you should keep in mind:

1. **Licensing Issues**: With cloud gaming, games are streamed rather than downloaded. This raises questions about the licensing agreements between developers and service providers. Are the licenses sufficient to cover streaming rights, or do they need revisions?

2. **Consumer Protection**: You deserve transparency regarding service levels and data usage as a player. Regulatory bodies must guarantee that consumers are adequately informed about their rights, especially regarding potential service interruptions and data management.

3. **Cross-border Regulations**: Cloud gaming often involves international servers, creating complications in a jurisdiction. Different countries may have varying laws on content distribution, user data, and consumer rights, which complicates provider compliance.

In traversing these complex regulatory waters, you'll find that balancing innovation with legal frameworks is vital.

As cloud gaming continues to expand, understanding these concerns will enhance your experience and empower you to advocate for a more transparent and fair gaming environment.

It's important to stay informed and involved as the industry evolves, guaranteeing that your rights as a gamer are protected in this new digital frontier.

Data storage and cybersecurity in gaming

The rapid growth of cloud gaming raises regulatory questions and highlights the significance of data storage and cybersecurity in the gaming industry. Companies must prioritize protecting sensitive user data as players increasingly rely on online platforms to access their favorite games.

With personal information, payment details, and in-game assets at stake, the potential for data breaches can have significant repercussions for both players and developers.

You need to be aware that gaming companies face a myriad of legal obligations regarding data protection. Compliance with regulations like the General Data Protection Regulation (GDPR) in Europe and the California Consumer Privacy Act (CCPA) in the U.S. is vital.

These laws require businesses to implement strict data storage protocols and guarantee that players' personal information is collected, processed, and stored securely. Failure to comply can result in hefty fines and damage a company's reputation.

Moreover, cybersecurity threats such as DDoS attacks, phishing scams, and malware pose constant risks. Developers should invest in robust security measures—such as encryption, secure servers, and regular vulnerability assessments—to safeguard their platforms against these threats.

Educating players about safe practices, such as using strong passwords and recognizing phishing attempts, is also significant.

Biometrics and personalization in gaming platforms

Incorporating biometrics into gaming platforms offers a transformative approach to personalization, enhancing user experience while raising important privacy concerns. By leveraging biometric data like facial recognition, fingerprint scanning, and voice recognition, gaming companies can create tailored experiences that adapt to your preferences and behaviors. However, this innovation isn't without its challenges.

You might find yourself grappling with the following emotional dilemmas:

1. **Trust Issues**: Can you trust gaming companies to responsibly handle your biometric data?

2. **Privacy Invasion**: Are you comfortable with your personal data being tracked and stored?

3. **Identity Security**: What happens if your biometric data gets compromised?

The gaming industry must navigate these complexities carefully. While personalization can enhance engagement and satisfaction, it also requires a commitment to safeguarding your sensitive information.

Developers must establish transparent policies informing you about how your data will be used, stored, and protected.

Moreover, legal frameworks are still catching up to technology. Current laws mightn't fully encompass the nuances of biometric data usage in gaming, creating potential liabilities for companies that don't comply with emerging regulations.

As a gamer, you should stay informed about these issues, as they directly affect your experience and security. Balancing the benefits of personalization with the need for robust privacy protections will be essential in shaping the future of gaming law and technology.

Impact of 5G and Mobile Gaming Expansion

With the rollout of 5G technology, mobile gaming is poised for a significant alteration that promises to enhance accessibility and performance. This shift from 4G to 5G is set to reduce latency dramatically and increase data transfer speeds, allowing for seamless gameplay experiences even in high-stakes environments.

You'll find that real-time multiplayer gaming becomes smoother, with lag reduced to a minimum, transforming how you connect with other players globally.

As mobile gaming expands, developers can create more complex and visually stunning games that were previously limited by network capabilities. The increased bandwidth of 5G enables richer graphics and more intricate game mechanics, encouraging innovation in game design.

Consequently, you'll see a surge in augmented reality (AR) and virtual reality (VR) applications, as these technologies require high-speed connections to function effectively.

Moreover, the broad availability of 5G networks opens up gaming to a wider audience. Those in rural or underserved areas can finally enjoy high-quality mobile gaming experiences, breaking down barriers that once restricted access.

This democratization of gaming raises important legal considerations, particularly concerning data privacy and consumer protection. As more players engage with mobile platforms, ensuring their rights and safety becomes paramount.

Digital contracts and smart contracts

Digital contracts and smart contracts are transforming the landscape of agreements in gaming and beyond. As a gamer or industry professional, you might feel the excitement of a new era where transactions become more efficient, transparent, and secure.

These digital agreements leverage blockchain technology to guarantee that both parties uphold their end of the deal, minimizing disputes and enhancing trust.

Consider these key advantages of digital contracts and smart contracts:

1. **Immediate Execution**: Smart contracts execute automatically when predefined conditions are met, eliminating delays and guaranteeing swift agreement completion.

2. **Reduced Costs**: By eliminating intermediaries, you can save money on legal fees and administrative expenses, making gaming investments more viable for smaller developers.

3. **Enhanced Security**: The decentralized nature of blockchain technology protects your agreements from tampering and fraud, providing peace of mind in a digital landscape often plagued by security concerns.

However, embracing these innovations requires you to remain aware of the legal implications.

The enforceability of digital contracts can vary by jurisdiction, and the evolving nature of cryptocurrency regulations adds layers of complexity. Thus, understanding the legal environment is significant before diving fully into these technologies.

Automation and IP in user-generated content

As gaming continues evolving through technologies like smart contracts, automating user-generated content (UGC) processes raises important questions about intellectual property (IP) rights. You might wonder how these advancements impact the ownership and distribution of content players create.

With automation, UGC can be rapidly generated, shared, and monetized, complicating traditional notions of IP. When you create content within a game, the platform often retains certain rights over that creation, which may contradict your expectations of ownership.

Automated systems can generate derivative works or modify assets without fully recognizing your contributions, leading to potential disputes over IP rights. You need to be aware that the terms of service for many gaming platforms can delegate rights away from the creator, which can be particularly concerning in an automated environment.

Moreover, integrating AI in UGC creation can further blur the lines of authorship. If an AI system modifies or enhances your creation, it questions who holds the IP rights—the creator, the AI developer, or the gaming platform?

Maneuvering through these issues requires a clear understanding of the legal frameworks governing IP and the specific terms associated with the platforms you engage with. Ultimately, as automation continues to shape the gaming landscape, you must stay informed about how these changes affect your rights as a creator.

International issues in cross-border tech gaming

Cross-border tech gaming presents many international challenges that can complicate compliance and enforcement of laws. As you navigate this complex landscape, you'll find that differing regulations and standards create a patchwork of legal requirements. This can lead to uncertainty and risk for developers and players alike.

Consider these critical issues that arise in cross-border tech gaming:

1. **Jurisdictional Conflicts**: Different countries have varying laws governing gaming, from taxation to consumer protection. This inconsistency can create confusion, as a game in one jurisdiction may be illegal in another.

2. **Data Privacy Regulations**: With the rise of global gaming platforms, varying data protection laws complicate how user data is collected, stored, and used. Non-compliance could lead to hefty fines and damage reputations.

3. **Intellectual Property Disputes**: As games cross borders, IP laws may clash. What's protected in one country mightn't be in another, leading to potential infringement issues that can stifle innovation.

These challenges underscore the necessity for developers and stakeholders to remain vigilant and informed.

You'll need to prioritize understanding the legal frameworks in each market you enter to minimize risks. By doing so, you can better navigate the intricacies of international gaming law and guarantee a more robust compliance strategy.

Ultimately, tackling these issues can pave the way for a more cohesive and thriving global gaming environment.

Fraud detection technology and privacy

Steering through the complexities of international gaming laws also highlights the need for effective fraud detection technologies, particularly about user privacy. As gaming platforms expand globally, they face increasing threats from fraudulent activities, including money laundering and account hacking. Implementing advanced fraud detection systems is essential for safeguarding both the gaming environment's integrity and users' data.

However, while deploying these technologies, you must also navigate the intricate balance between fraud prevention and privacy rights. Users expect their personal information to be protected, yet the data collected for fraud detection often includes sensitive details. Transparency becomes imperative; you must clarify how data is collected, processed, and stored. Providing users with information about these practices fosters trust and aligns your operations with various privacy regulations, such as the General Data Protection Regulation (GDPR) in Europe.

Moreover, effective fraud detection shouldn't compromise user anonymity. Techniques like machine learning can help identify patterns indicative of fraud without exposing individual user information. This approach allows you to uphold user privacy while effectively mitigating risks associated with fraudulent behavior.

AI moderation in gaming communities

AI moderation transforms how gaming communities maintain order and foster a positive environment. By employing advanced algorithms, gaming platforms can efficiently identify and address toxic behavior, allowing players to enjoy their experience without disruption. This technology streamlines moderation and empowers community managers to focus on engagement rather than policing.

Consider these key emotional impacts of AI moderation:

1. **Safety and Security**: With AI monitoring chat and interactions, players feel safer knowing that harmful language or behavior is swiftly dealt with, creating a welcoming atmosphere.

2. **Community Trust**: When players see that moderation is consistent and fair, they trust the platform. This trust encourages more interaction and collaboration among players, strengthening the community.

3. **Enhanced Gameplay Experience**: AI moderation allows for a more enjoyable gaming experience by minimizing toxic interactions. Players can focus on the game itself rather than maneuvering through a hostile environment.

The implications of AI moderation extend beyond immediate conflict resolution. They reshape the cultural landscape of gaming communities, fostering inclusivity and respect.

As these technologies evolve, they'll continue to influence not just how we play but also how we connect with one another. However, it's essential to maintain a balance, ensuring that AI doesn't infringe on free speech or stifle creativity.

Predictive algorithms and behavioral analytics

Many gaming companies increasingly rely on predictive algorithms and behavioral analytics to enhance player experiences and optimize engagement strategies. By analyzing player data, you can identify patterns and preferences, allowing you to tailor content and promotional offers that resonate with your audience. This targeted approach boosts player retention and drives monetization efforts, making it imperative for staying competitive in the industry.

Predictive algorithms enable you to forecast player behavior, such as when they're likely to churn or what in-game purchases they might make. Understanding these trends allows you to intervene proactively, offering incentives or personalized experiences that keep players engaged. For instance, if your data indicates a player is losing interest, you can send them tailored promotions or re-engagement campaigns to draw them back in.

Behavioral analytics also helps you understand the broader gaming landscape. By examining aggregated data, you can spot emerging trends, adjust game mechanics, and refine user interfaces to enhance usability. This data-driven approach guarantees your game remains relevant and enjoyable.

However, while utilizing these technologies, you must navigate the legalities of data privacy and player consent. Compliance with regulations like GDPR and CCPA is essential, as mishandling player data can lead to significant legal repercussions.

To foster trust and loyalty among your player base, you need to balance innovation with ethical considerations. Leveraging predictive algorithms and behavioral analytics, you must also consider these legal frameworks for sustainable success in the gaming industry.

Technology's impact on future regulations

As technology continues to evolve, it's reshaping not just gameplay but also the regulatory landscape surrounding the gaming industry. You're witnessing a notable shift where regulatory frameworks must adapt to keep pace with innovations like virtual reality, blockchain, and artificial intelligence. These technologies are enhancing user experience but also presenting new challenges for regulators.

Consider the implications of these advancements:

1. **Data Privacy**: With more data being collected than ever, how will regulations protect players' personal information?

2. **Fair Play**: As algorithms dictate game outcomes, what measures will guarantee fairness and transparency in gaming?

3. **Accessibility**: As gaming technology advances, how will regulators guarantee equal access for all players?

Each of these concerns requires a thoughtful legal response. Regulatory bodies must engage with technologists and industry leaders to develop guidelines safeguarding players while fostering innovation.

Future regulations must address existing challenges and anticipate new issues that arise as technology becomes even more integrated into gaming experiences.

Moreover, as online gaming expands globally, you can expect a patchwork of regulations that vary greatly from one jurisdiction to another. This inconsistency can lead to confusion and potential exploitation.

As a result, the collaboration between technology developers and legal experts is essential in establishing a coherent regulatory framework that adapts to ongoing technological changes. In this evolving landscape, staying informed and proactive will be key to guaranteeing a fair and responsible gaming environment.

Chapter Seven

eSports and Competitive Gaming Law

As esports grows into a global powerhouse, you might wonder about the legal framework that supports this thriving industry. It's not just about the games; it's about tournament regulations, player rights, and the complex web of sponsorship agreements. Understanding these legalities is essential for anyone involved in competitive gaming. But what happens when disputes arise or when player rights are challenged? The answers to these questions could greatly impact the future of esports, and you'll want to explore the implications further.

Growth and Significance of eSports Worldwide

The growth of eSports worldwide has transformed the gaming landscape into a multi-billion-dollar industry, capturing the attention of both players and investors alike. You might notice that this surge isn't just about popularity; it reflects a significant shift in how society views competitive gaming. Events like the League of Legends World Championship and The International draw millions of viewers, showcasing the potential of eSports as a legitimate form of entertainment.

As a gamer or even an investor, you should recognize the implications of this growth. The audience for eSports continues to expand, with demographics shifting to include not just younger individuals but also a diverse array of age groups and backgrounds. This broadening appeal has led to increased sponsorship opportunities, partnerships with major brands, and substantial media rights deals, all contributing to the industry's financial success.

Moreover, the infrastructure surrounding eSports is evolving. Dedicated arenas, professional teams, and collegiate leagues emerge, further legitimizing competitive gaming as a career path. This professionalization allows players to pursue gaming full-time, fostering a culture of dedication and skill development.

In your analysis of eSports, consider its global reach. Countries across continents are embracing eSports, hosting events, and featuring national teams, which enhances the competitive spirit and cultural exchange.

As you explore this dynamic field, it becomes evident that eSports' significance extends beyond entertainment; it's shaping economies, cultures, and the future of gaming itself.

Legal Requirements for eSports Tournaments

Maneuvering the legal landscape is essential for organizing successful eSports tournaments. You must grasp various legal requirements to guarantee compliance and avoid pitfalls.

First, consider the licensing for the games involved. Many titles have specific terms of use, and failure to adhere to these can lead to legal disputes or the cancellation of your event. Always secure the necessary permissions from game publishers.

Next, consider the venue. If you're hosting in a physical location, verify that it meets local regulations regarding safety, accessibility, and occupancy limits. You'll also need to acquire the appropriate permits for hosting a public event, which can vary considerably by jurisdiction.

Don't overlook the importance of participant agreements. Clearly outlining rules, prize distributions, and conduct expectations in extensive terms of service can protect you legally and guarantee a smooth tournament. These agreements should also address intellectual property rights, especially concerning streaming and broadcasting the event.

Moreover, if your tournament involves cash prizes, familiarize yourself with local gambling laws. Certain jurisdictions may classify prize pools as gambling, which could require additional licenses.

Protecting player rights in eSports

Protecting player rights in eSports is just as significant as meeting legal requirements for tournaments. Players often find themselves in complex contractual relationships with organizations, sponsors, and publishers, which can lead to exploitation or unfair treatment.

It is important to establish clear guidelines that outline players' rights regarding compensation, personal data protection, and working conditions.

First, fair compensation and revenue sharing should be prioritized. Many players face substantial risks by investing time and resources into their careers. Hence, organizations must guarantee that contracts provide equitable pay and transparent revenue-sharing models. This fosters a sustainable environment that respects player contributions.

Next, safeguarding personal data is fundamental. Players often share sensitive information with teams and sponsors, creating vulnerabilities to data breaches. Legislation like the General Data Protection Regulation (GDPR) emphasizes the significance of protecting personal data. Organizations should implement robust data protection protocols to guarantee players' information remains secure.

Additionally, fostering a healthy competitive environment is essential. This includes addressing issues like harassment and discrimination. Establishing a clear code of conduct and an accessible reporting mechanism empowers players to voice concerns without fear of retaliation.

Sponsorship and endorsement regulations

Sponsorship and endorsement regulations are essential in shaping the esports landscape and influencing how players, teams, and organizations engage with brands. As the industry grows, these regulations guarantee that agreements between sponsors and esports entities are transparent and fair. They also protect the interests of the involved parties and maintain the integrity of the competitive gaming environment.

When working with sponsors, players must know the legal implications of endorsements. Contracts often include clauses that dictate the use of logos, the duration of the partnership, and the nature of promotional activities. You'll need to understand how intellectual property rights apply to your brand collaborations, as misuse can lead to significant legal repercussions.

Moreover, compliance with advertising standards is critical. Players and teams must navigate a maze of regulations that govern what can be promoted and how. For instance, if a sponsor markets products that target minors, there are strict guidelines to follow, especially in esports, where younger audiences are prevalent.

Additionally, disclosures regarding sponsored content are mandatory in many jurisdictions. Failure to adhere to these requirements can result in penalties and damage to your credibility.

As you engage with sponsorships, keeping abreast of these regulations will not only shield you from legal issues but also enhance your professional reputation within the esports community. Understanding these regulations is key to leveraging sponsorship opportunities effectively in a dynamic industry like esports.

Media rights and broadcasting considerations

Media rights and broadcasting considerations are fundamental for the growth and sustainability of the esports ecosystem. As you navigate this landscape, you'll find that these rights dictate how esports events are shared with audiences worldwide. The value of media rights lies in their ability to generate revenue, attract sponsors, and build a fanbase. Understanding these rights can greatly influence your strategic decisions in the gaming industry.

When negotiating media rights, you must consider the various platforms available for broadcasting. Traditional television networks, streaming services, and social media platforms offer unique advantages and challenges. Each platform has its audience demographics and engagement metrics, which can impact your choice of media partner. Assessing which platform aligns best with your target audience and goals is important.

Licensing agreements are another key component. They establish the terms under which content can be broadcasted, including exclusivity, duration, and territorial rights. You'll want to confirm these agreements protect your interests while fostering partnerships that enhance your brand's visibility.

Moreover, intellectual property rights play a critical role. You need to verify that the content produced during esports events doesn't infringe on copyright or trademark protections. This aspect requires careful attention to detail, especially when using game footage or player likenesses.

Gambling and betting in eSports competitions

Gambling and betting in esports competitions have rapidly gained traction, drawing excitement and concern within the gaming community. As a participant or observer in this burgeoning landscape, you must maneuver through the complex legalities governing these activities. Various jurisdictions approach esports betting differently, creating a patchwork of regulations that can complicate your involvement.

In many regions, betting on esports is treated similarly to traditional sports betting. This means you'd need to be aware of your local gambling authorities' legal age restrictions and licensing requirements. Online platforms have emerged, providing bettors access to various esports events, yet not all are regulated, leading to potential risks. Understanding which platforms operate legally can protect you from fraudulent sites.

Moreover, the rise of in-game betting—where you can wager on specific game outcomes or player performances—adds another layer of complexity. While it can enhance your viewing experience, it also raises questions about integrity and the potential for match-fixing. Authorities are increasingly scrutinizing these practices to guarantee fair play.

As the esports betting landscape evolves, so does the conversation around responsible gambling. You should consider the implications of your betting habits, as they can affect your finances and the broader community.

Keeping informed about the legal framework surrounding esports gambling helps you stay compliant and contributes to a healthier gaming environment. Ultimately, maneuvering through this space requires diligence and awareness, guaranteeing that your engagement remains exciting and responsible.

Team contracts and player obligations

In the competitive domain of esports, team contracts, and player obligations are fundamental components that define the relationship between players and organizations. These contracts serve as formal agreements that outline both parties' responsibilities, expectations, and rights. As a player, you need to understand that signing a contract isn't merely a formality; it's a commitment that can greatly influence your career trajectory.

Typically, a team contract will specify your role within the organization, including participating in tournaments, practice schedules, and promotional activities. It's essential to be aware of clauses related to performance expectations, as failure to meet these can lead to penalties, including termination.

You'll also find clauses that dictate how revenue is shared, which can include prize money, sponsorship earnings, and streaming revenue. Therefore, it's important to guarantee you're comfortable with these terms.

Moreover, player obligations often extend beyond gameplay. You may be required to maintain a certain level of public conduct, as your behavior can reflect on the team's brand. Compliance with rules regarding social media engagement and communication with fans becomes critical, as breaches might result in disciplinary actions.

Understanding the legal language in these contracts is imperative. If necessary, seek legal advice to guarantee that your interests are protected.

A well-structured contract can provide security and clarity, allowing you to focus on your performance while fostering a positive relationship with your organization.

Anti-doping policies in Competitive Gaming

As competitive gaming grows, implementing anti-doping policies has become vital to maintaining fair play and integrity within esports. Like traditional sports, the competitive gaming scene faces challenges related to performance-enhancing substances. The rise in professionalism among players necessitates rigorous standards to guarantee that competition remains fair and that the athletes' health is prioritized.

You might be surprised to learn that many esports organizations have started adopting anti-doping regulations, often modeled after those established by the World Anti-Doping Agency (WADA). These policies outline prohibited substances and methods, testing protocols, and the consequences of violations. By adhering to these guidelines, esports leagues can promote a level playing field, ultimately enhancing the industry's credibility.

Moreover, anti-doping policies help protect players from the pressures to use banned substances to enhance performance. With stakes increasingly high in tournaments, the temptation to resort to unfair advantages can become significant. Implementing these policies signals a commitment to athlete welfare and the sport's integrity.

However, the complexity arises when considering the diverse range of games and their unique demands. Each game may require tailored approaches to address specific performance-enhancing techniques.

Understanding the nuances of anti-doping regulations will be vital for players, teams, and organizations as they navigate this evolving landscape. By fostering an environment of accountability, these policies contribute to a healthier and more respected competitive gaming ecosystem.

Regulation of in-game cheating and doping

Addressing in-game cheating and doping is essential for preserving the integrity of esports competitions. As you immerse yourself in competitive gaming, you'll notice that these issues can undermine fair play and skew results. Regulatory bodies and game developers must establish clear guidelines and enforce strict penalties to combat these practices effectively.

Consider the following aspects of regulation:

- **Detection Technologies**: Utilizing advanced software to identify cheating methods, such as aimbots or wallhacks, can help maintain a level playing field.

- **Player Education**: Teaching players about the consequences of cheating and doping can foster a culture of integrity within the community.

- **Standardized Regulations**: Creating uniform rules across different games and tournaments can simplify enforcement and reduce confusion among players.

- **Collaboration with Developers**: Regulatory bodies should work closely with game developers to guarantee that games are designed with built-in anti-cheat mechanisms.

When these components are integrated, you can see how they collectively contribute to a safer and more equitable competitive environment.

Gamers need to understand that the repercussions of cheating extend beyond personal penalties; they can damage the reputation of the entire esports community. By advocating for stringent regulations and promoting a culture of fair play, you can help safeguard the future of esports and ensure that competitions remain a true test of skill and strategy.

IP issues with eSports content creation

With the rise of esports, content creation has become a significant avenue for engagement and revenue generation. However, this burgeoning field faces intricate intellectual property (IP) issues that you must navigate. As a content creator, understanding the legal landscape of IP rights is essential for safeguarding your work and avoiding potential pitfalls.

When you create content featuring gameplay, characters, and other elements from existing games, you risk infringing on the copyright of the game developers. These developers hold exclusive rights to their intellectual property, and unauthorized use can lead to takedown notices or even legal action.

To mitigate this risk, familiarize yourself with fair use principles. These principles may allow you to use certain elements without permission but remember that fair use isn't a blanket protection and is often determined by the context of your content.

Additionally, trademarks play a significant role in the esports ecosystem. Logos, team names, and branding are typically trademarked, and using them without permission can lead to trademark infringement claims. Always seek permission or use generic alternatives if unsure about the rights associated with specific elements.

Furthermore, consider licensing agreements with game developers or publishers. These agreements can clarify your rights and responsibilities, allowing you to create content while respecting the IP holders' interests.

Ultimately, staying informed and proactive about IP issues will empower you to thrive in the competitive world of esports content creation.

Contract law in player and team relationships

In today's fast-evolving esports landscape, understanding contract law is essential for players and teams to establish clear expectations and protect their interests. Contracts are the backbone of player-team relationships, outlining roles, responsibilities, and compensation.

When you're involved in esports, you'll encounter various contracts, including player agreements, sponsorship deals, and endorsement contracts. Each one carries its own legal implications and requires careful attention.

Key elements of these contracts often include:

- **Compensation Structure**: Details on salary, bonuses, and revenue-sharing.

- **Duration**: The length of the contract and conditions for renewal or termination.

- **Performance Metrics**: Expectations regarding gameplay, attendance, and training obligations.

- **Intellectual Property Rights**: Provisions using team branding and player likeness.

Navigating these contracts can be complex; misunderstanding even a single clause can lead to disputes and financial losses.

As a player or team manager, it's vital that you take the time to read and comprehend every aspect of the agreement. Seeking legal advice before signing can help you identify red flags and negotiate terms that align with your goals.

As the esports industry continues to grow, the legal frameworks surrounding these contracts will also evolve, making it imperative for all parties to stay informed and proactive in their contractual dealings.

Legal battles over eSports tournament winnings

Contracts not only define relationships but also set the stage for potential disputes, especially when it comes to tournament winnings. In the fast-paced world of esports, the stakes and tensions surrounding prize distributions are high. When you participate in a tournament, you likely sign a contract outlining your involvement's terms, including how winnings are allocated.

However, discrepancies can arise, leading to legal battles that can be both costly and time-consuming. One common issue involves disputes over the interpretation of contract clauses. For instance, you might find yourself in a situation where an ambiguous term leads to differing opinions on how winnings should be divided among team members. In these cases, courts often look at the intent behind the contract, which can complicate matters further.

Another significant factor is the enforcement of tournament rules, which can vary widely between organizers. If a tournament organizer fails to adhere to their rules or changes them mid-competition, you might've grounds for a legal claim over your winnings.

Additionally, disputes can emerge from sponsorship agreements tied to tournament performance. If a sponsor's payout is contingent upon your team's placement, and there's disagreement on how that placement is determined, you could end up in a legal quagmire.

Ultimately, understanding the intricacies of these contracts and the legal implications of tournament winnings is vital for you as a player, ensuring you're better prepared to navigate any disputes that may arise.

Labor laws and compensation for players

Many players in the esports industry find themselves maneuvering complex labor laws that impact their compensation and working conditions. Understanding these legal frameworks can be essential for your career. Unlike traditional sports, the esports scene is still evolving, and many players may not realize the implications of their contracts, which can greatly affect their financial stability.

Here are some key factors that shape labor laws and compensation in esports:

- **Contractual Obligations**: Many players sign contracts that lack clarity, often leading to disputes over salary, bonuses, and revenue-sharing arrangements.

- **Employment Status**: Players may be classified as independent contractors or employees, affecting benefits like health insurance, retirement plans, and job security.

- **Minimum Wage Laws**: Depending on your location, local minimum wage laws may not apply to esports players, meaning some may earn below living wage standards.

- **Collective Bargaining**: The absence of unions in esports limits your capacity to collectively negotiate better working conditions and compensation.

Navigating these complexities requires diligence and an understanding of your rights. As esports gains recognition, the need for standardized labor laws and fair compensation will likely increase.

Keeping informed about these issues helps you advocate for your rights and sets the groundwork for a more equitable industry.

Dispute resolution in eSports

Disputes in esports can arise from various sources, including contract misunderstandings and competition regulations. As a participant or stakeholder in this fast-evolving industry, it's important to understand the mechanisms for resolving these disputes effectively.

Many esports organizations and tournaments have established dispute resolution procedures, often including mediation and arbitration clauses in player contracts. These clauses can expedite the process and minimize costs but require you to relinquish your right to pursue traditional litigation.

When a dispute occurs, the specific contracts involved must be reviewed. Often, these documents outline the preferred methods for resolution, whether through internal review boards or third-party arbitration services.

If you're involved in an esports league, familiarize yourself with the league's rules and the procedures for addressing grievances. This knowledge can provide you with a clear pathway for resolution.

Moreover, effective communication is significant. Engaging in open dialogue with the other party can often resolve misunderstandings before they escalate into formal disputes.

If necessary, don't hesitate to seek advice from legal professionals experienced in esports law. They can provide informed guidance tailored to your specific situation.

Future of regulation in eSports and its growth

As esports continues to expand exponentially, the need for thorough regulation becomes increasingly crucial. The industry is evolving rapidly, and without appropriate legal frameworks, the potential for issues like fraud, player exploitation, and unfair competition rises.

You'll witness a growing trend toward establishing clearer guidelines and standards that promote fairness and protect players, organizations, and fans alike.

Here are some key aspects shaping the future of esports regulation:

- **Player Rights**: Ensuring fair contracts and protections against exploitation will be paramount as players gain more visibility and leverage.

- **Age Restrictions**: As esports attracts younger audiences, regulations around age restrictions for participation and viewership will become more essential.

- **Sponsorship and Advertising**: Clear guidelines will emerge regarding sponsorship deals, especially concerning minors and ethical advertising practices.

- **Integrity and Anti-Cheating Measures**: Strengthening regulations to combat cheating and match-fixing will help maintain the integrity of competitions.

With regulatory bodies starting to engage with this dynamic landscape, you can expect to see a blend of traditional sports laws and innovative approaches tailored to esports' unique challenges.

The future may also involve international cooperation, as esports transcend borders. As regulations evolve, it's crucial for all stakeholders—players, organizers, and fans—to stay informed and adapt to these changes.

In doing so, you'll help foster a thriving, sustainable esports ecosystem that benefits everyone involved.

Chapter Eight

Global Gaming and Cross-Border Regulations

When you think about global gaming, it's clear that cross-border regulations create a labyrinth of challenges for operators. Each jurisdiction has its own licensing, taxation, and compliance laws, which can complicate even the simplest transactions. As new technologies emerge, the legal landscape evolves, raising questions about consumer protection and data privacy. Understanding these complexities isn't just beneficial; it's essential for survival in this competitive industry. So, how can businesses effectively navigate this intricate web to guarantee compliance and foster growth? The answers might surprise you.

Gaming laws across continents: a comparative view

As you explore the gaming laws across continents, you'll quickly notice significant variations in regulatory frameworks and enforcement practices.

In North America, particularly the United States, the legal landscape is fragmented, with each state having its rules governing gaming. Some states embrace broad legalization, fostering vibrant gaming markets, while others maintain strict prohibitions. This patchwork creates challenges for operators who wish to navigate compliance effectively.

In contrast, Europe offers a more unified approach, although individual countries still wield considerable authority over gaming regulations. The European Union has made strides toward harmonization, yet disparities remain, especially regarding online gaming. Countries like the United Kingdom have established robust regulatory bodies, such as the UK Gambling Commission, which sets high standards for consumer protection and integrity in gaming.

Asia presents a different scenario, where gaming laws often blend traditional cultural values with modern regulatory practices. Countries like Macau and Singapore have developed extensive legal frameworks to manage and promote gaming tourism, attracting global operators while ensuring responsible gaming practices.

The gaming industry is rapidly evolving in Africa, with nations like South Africa implementing thorough regulations to oversee both land-based and online gaming. However, enforcement remains inconsistent across the continent, leading to a landscape where illegal gambling flourishes in some regions.

Understanding these regional differences is significant for anyone looking to engage with the global gaming market. You must adapt your strategies to navigate these diverse legal environments effectively.

Key challenges of cross-border regulations

Maneuvering the complexities of cross-border regulations in the gaming industry presents significant challenges for operators.

First, you'll encounter the diversity of laws across jurisdictions. Each country has its own regulatory framework, which can differ drastically regarding licensing, taxation, and compliance requirements. This inconsistency makes it difficult to develop a uniform operational strategy, forcing you to adapt to multiple legal landscapes.

Next, you're likely to face issues related to enforcement. Even if you comply with one jurisdiction's regulations, you might still be vulnerable to legal action from another. This risk stems from the varying degrees of enforcement and the often ambiguous nature of international law, which can expose you to penalties and litigation.

Additionally, the rapid evolution of technology presents a challenge. As new gaming platforms and digital currencies emerge, existing regulations may lag behind, leading to uncertainty. You need to stay ahead of the curve, but the pace of change can be overwhelming.

Then there's the issue of consumer protection. Different regions prioritize player safety and privacy in varying degrees. To build trust with your customers, you must navigate these differing expectations carefully.

Lastly, political considerations can't be overlooked. Changes in government policies or international relations can dramatically affect regulatory environments. This volatility adds another layer of complexity when making strategic decisions.

International trade and gaming legalities

Steering international trade in the gaming industry involves a complex web of legalities that can greatly impact your operations. Each country has its own set of laws governing gaming activities, from licensing requirements to taxation policies. Understanding these regulations is imperative to navigate the global landscape effectively.

First, consider the implications of varying legal frameworks. For instance, some jurisdictions may require operators to obtain local licenses before offering services, while others might've more lenient regulations. You must conduct thorough research to guarantee compliance with local laws to expand into a new market. Failing to do so could result in fines or even suspending your operations.

Additionally, trade agreements can play a considerable role in the gaming industry. Countries involved in favorable trade agreements may allow smoother entry and operations, while those with restrictive policies can hinder your ability to compete internationally. You should also know how currency fluctuations and taxation affect your profits in cross-border transactions.

Another essential aspect is consumer protection laws, which can vary greatly between regions. It is fundamental to ensure that your gaming practices align with local expectations regarding fairness, transparency, and responsible gaming to maintain your reputation and avoid legal pitfalls.

Protecting IP across jurisdictions

Steering through the complexities of protecting intellectual property (IP) across jurisdictions is vital for gaming companies looking to safeguard their innovations and creative assets. As you expand your reach globally, understanding the nuances of IP laws in different territories becomes essential.

Each jurisdiction has its own regulations regarding copyrights, trademarks, patents, and trade secrets, making it imperative to develop a tailored strategy for each market.

You need to start by identifying your IP assets and determining how they're protected in various regions. For instance, while copyright may automatically protect your game software in many countries, you may need to register trademarks to secure your brand identity more robustly.

In addition, the scope of protection can vary greatly; what's enforceable in one country may not be in another, exposing you to risks such as infringement or unauthorized use.

Engaging local legal experts familiar with the gaming sector can provide invaluable insights into effective IP strategies. They can guide you on the best practices for enforcing your rights and steering the registration processes.

Additionally, you should consider the impact of international treaties, like the Berne Convention or the TRIPS Agreement, as they can offer a framework for protecting your IP across borders.

Cross-border compliance in online gaming

Maneuvering the intricacies of cross-border compliance in online gaming is vital for companies operating in multiple jurisdictions. Understanding the varying legal frameworks becomes essential as you expand your gaming operations internationally. Different countries have distinct laws governing online gaming, including licensing requirements, taxation, and consumer protection regulations. You must guarantee that your operations align with these diverse regulations to avoid legal pitfalls.

One key aspect of cross-border compliance is obtaining the necessary licenses. Each jurisdiction may require you to secure separate permits, and the criteria for approval can vary considerably. For example, some regions may impose stringent regulations regarding responsible gaming measures, while others focus on the technical standards of your gaming software.

You should invest time and resources to navigate these licensing processes effectively.

Taxation is another vital factor in cross-border compliance. Many jurisdictions impose specific taxes on online gaming revenues, and failing to adhere to these requirements can result in hefty penalties. Understanding the tax implications in each market where you operate is essential to guarantee that your financial practices comply with local laws.

Lastly, consumer protection regulations are increasingly becoming a focal point for regulators globally. You must implement robust measures to protect user data and promote responsible gaming practices. By prioritizing compliance in these areas, you mitigate legal risks, enhance your company's reputation, and build trust with your players.

This approach can set you apart from others who may overlook these vital aspects in the competitive online gaming landscape.

Regional restrictions and geo-blocking

Regional restrictions and geo-blocking are vital components in online gaming that can greatly impact your operations. These measures are designed to comply with varying legal frameworks across different jurisdictions, shaping who can access your games and services. Understanding these concepts is essential for your business strategy.

Here are key points to reflect on:

- **Legal Compliance**: Adhering to local laws regarding gaming can prevent hefty fines or legal action.

- **Market Access**: Regional restrictions can limit your audience, affecting potential revenue streams.

- **User Experience**: Geo-blocking can frustrate users who travel or relocate, impacting customer loyalty.

- **Technology**: Implementing geo-blocking requires sophisticated technology to accurately identify user locations.

- **Competition**: Understanding regional constraints helps you navigate competitive landscapes and identify opportunities.

While geo-blocking can help mitigate legal risks, it can also create barriers that may alienate potential players. You have to strike a balance between compliance and accessibility.

As regulations evolve, staying informed about regional laws and restrictions becomes even more vital. Failing to do so could lead to unintentional violations, costing you reputation and revenue.

Anti-money laundering in global operations

Regional restrictions and geo-blocking aren't the only legal challenges online gaming companies face; anti-money laundering (AML) regulations also play a significant role in global operations.

These regulations require you to implement strict measures to prevent the laundering of illicit funds through gaming platforms. Non-compliance can lead to severe penalties, including hefty fines and loss of licenses, which can jeopardize your business.

To effectively navigate AML regulations, you must understand the requirements specific to each jurisdiction you operate. This often involves conducting thorough customer due diligence (CDD), which includes verifying identities and monitoring transactions for suspicious activity.

You'll also need to maintain detailed records of these processes, ensuring they can withstand regulatory scrutiny.

Moreover, developing an effective risk assessment strategy is vital. Different markets present varying levels of risk, and you must tailor your AML policies accordingly.

Regular staff training on compliance practices is also essential, as employees are on the front lines of identifying and reporting potential money laundering activities.

Managing international partnerships

Successful management of international partnerships in the gaming industry hinges on a clear understanding of diverse regulatory landscapes and cultural nuances.

As you navigate these complexities, you'll find that effective collaboration requires more than legal compliance. You must also cultivate relationships built on trust and mutual benefit.

To excel in managing these partnerships, consider the following key strategies:

- **Research Local Regulations**: Familiarize yourself with the gaming laws and regulations in each partner's jurisdiction to avoid legal pitfalls.

- **Cultural Sensitivity**: Understand and respect cultural differences that may influence business practices and communication styles.

- **Transparent Communication**: Maintain open lines of communication to foster trust and clarify expectations among all partners.

- **Risk Management**: Develop a thorough risk assessment strategy to proactively identify and mitigate potential challenges.

- **Shared Objectives**: Align your goals with your international partners to create a cohesive and cooperative working environment.

Import/export laws for gaming equipment

Maneuvering import/export laws for gaming equipment can be complex, especially as regulations vary considerably across countries.

You'll need to familiarize yourself with the laws of both the importing and exporting countries, as non-compliance can result in hefty fines or confiscation of goods. Each jurisdiction has its own set of regulations regarding what constitutes legal gaming equipment, which can include everything from physical devices to software.

First, identify the classification of the equipment you plan to import or export. Some countries might categorize gaming machines differently, affecting tariffs and import duties.

For instance, certain regions may require specific certifications or licenses before allowing the entry of gaming devices. You'll want to guarantee your products meet these requirements to avoid delays or penalties.

Next, consider the documentation necessary for the import/export process. This often includes invoices, packing lists, and certificates of origin, but you might require additional permits depending on the equipment.

Guarantee you're prepared to provide these documents to customs authorities.

Lastly, monitor legislative changes. The gaming industry is dynamic, and regulations can shift rapidly.

Staying informed about current laws guarantees compliance, and you can adapt your strategies accordingly. Regularly consult legal experts or trade compliance specialists specializing in gaming law to help navigate these complexities effectively.

Handling multi-jurisdictional licensing

Maneuvering the complexities of import/export laws sets the stage for understanding multi-jurisdictional licensing in the gaming industry. As you explore this intricate landscape, you'll find that maneuvering various regulatory frameworks is vital for compliance and operational success.

Each jurisdiction has its licensing requirements, which can vary greatly, impacting your ability to offer gaming services across borders.

To effectively handle multi-jurisdictional licensing, consider these key factors:

- **Understand local regulations**: Each jurisdiction has unique laws governing gaming operations.

- **Assess licensing fees**: Costs can vary widely; budgeting accurately is essential.

- **Stay updated on changes**: Regulations can shift, so remain vigilant to adapt your strategies.

- **Engage local experts**: Collaborating with legal advisors familiar with regional laws can streamline the process.

- **Implement compliance measures**: Establishing robust compliance protocols guarantees adherence to diverse regulations.

Cross-border data protection issues

Steering through cross-border data protection issues is essential as gaming companies expand their global reach. With players from different jurisdictions, you'll encounter varied legal frameworks governing data privacy. For instance, the General Data Protection Regulation (GDPR) in Europe sets stringent rules on how personal data is collected, processed, and stored, while other regions may have more lenient regulations. This inconsistency can lead to significant compliance challenges.

When you collect data from players in multiple countries, you must guarantee compliance with each jurisdiction's laws. If you fail, you risk facing hefty fines and damaging your reputation. Additionally, data breaches can lead to severe consequences, including legal action and loss of customer trust.

To protect sensitive information across borders, you need to implement robust data security measures, including encryption and regular audits.

You should also consider how data is transferred between regions. For example, the EU-US Privacy Shield framework has been invalidated, emphasizing the need for alternative legal mechanisms like Standard Contractual Clauses or Binding Corporate Rules. Understanding these tools is crucial for maintaining compliance while facilitating data flow.

Taxes, duties, and fees in global gaming

Maneuvering taxes, duties, and fees in global gaming can be complex due to the diverse regulatory landscapes across countries. Each jurisdiction has its own set of rules, and understanding these can be essential for compliance and profitability.

To navigate this intricate environment, you need to be aware of several key factors:

- **Tax Rates**: Different countries impose varying tax rates on gaming revenues.

- **Licensing Fees**: Obtaining necessary licenses can involve considerable upfront and ongoing costs.

- **Consumption Taxes**: Some nations apply taxes on gaming products, affecting pricing strategies.

- **Cross-Border Transactions**: Tax implications can arise from international transactions, complicating financial management.

- **Compliance Costs**: Ensuring adherence to local regulations may require legal and accounting services investment.

As you analyze the global gaming landscape, consider that these fiscal obligations can notably impact your bottom line. For instance, some countries might offer lower tax rates to attract operators, while others impose hefty fees that can deter entry.

Also, fluctuating exchange rates and political changes can further complicate financial planning.

Ultimately, your success in the global gaming market will depend on your ability to effectively manage these taxes, duties, and fees. Staying informed about regulation changes and fostering relationships with local authorities can also provide a competitive advantage.

Enforcing judgments across borders

Maneuvering the complexities of enforcing judgments across borders is essential for businesses involved in the global gaming industry. When you operate in multiple jurisdictions, understanding how to enforce legal decisions can make or break your enterprise. Different countries have various legal frameworks and requirements for recognizing foreign judgments, and this variability complicates the enforcement process.

You'll find that some jurisdictions adhere to international treaties like the Hague Convention, which facilitates the recognition and enforcement of judgments. However, many countries remain outside these agreements, leaving you to navigate individual national laws. This inconsistency means that even if you win a case in one country, another country may refuse to recognize that victory, undermining your efforts.

Moreover, practical challenges arise. You might need to translate legal documents, hire local attorneys, or contend with cultural biases against foreign entities. Additionally, enforcement mechanisms, such as garnishing wages or seizing assets, might differ greatly, impacting the speed and efficacy of your actions.

In the gaming industry, where reputational risk is paramount, a failure to enforce a judgment can lead to considerable financial losses and damage to your brand. Consequently, it's critical to assess the enforceability of any judgment before pursuing cross-border litigation.

Understanding the nuances of each jurisdiction safeguards your interests and enhances your strategic positioning in the global market. You can effectively navigate these complexities and protect your business's legal rights by staying informed and proactive.

Online gambling and international treaties

International treaties that shape regulations and practices across borders heavily influence the landscape of online gambling. These treaties create frameworks that countries use to regulate online gambling activities, ensuring a degree of uniformity and fairness. However, they also present challenges, as differing national interests complicate enforcement and compliance.

Here are some key aspects of international treaties affecting online gambling:

- **Harmonization of Regulations**: Treaties often aim to standardize rules, making it easier for operators to navigate different jurisdictions.

- **Consumer Protection**: Many treaties emphasize the importance of safeguarding players, ensuring fair play, and responsible gaming.

- **Taxation Agreements**: Treaties can address tax implications for online gambling operators, reducing double taxation and fostering cooperation.

- **Cross-Border Enforcement**: They provide mechanisms for enforcing judgments and decisions across borders, which can be essential in resolving disputes.

- **Licensing and Operation**: International treaties can dictate operators' licensing requirements, helping legitimize the industry.

Understanding how these treaties function is fundamental for anyone involved in online gambling in this complex environment.

You must stay informed about the evolving legal landscape and recognize how these international agreements impact your operations.

As countries continue to negotiate and revise treaties, the interplay between national laws and international agreements will remain a significant factor in shaping the future of online gambling.

Adapting to this dynamic environment can position you for success in the global gaming market.

Case studies: Successes and Failures in Global Gaming Law

Case studies in global gaming law reveal a spectrum of successes and failures shaped by varying regulatory frameworks and compliance challenges.

One notable success story is regulating online gambling in the United Kingdom. The UK Gambling Commission's robust licensing and regulatory standards have fostered a safe environment for players and operators. This framework increased consumer protection and generated significant tax revenue for the government, proving that a well-structured legal environment can lead to thriving markets.

Conversely, the United States presents a mixed bag of outcomes. The repeal of PASPA in 2018 allowed states to legalize sports betting, yet the lack of a cohesive federal framework has resulted in a patchwork of regulations.

States like New Jersey have successfully implemented regulations that encourage market participation and protect consumers, while others struggle with inconsistent laws that hinder growth and create confusion among operators.

Another example lies in the failure of unregulated markets, such as in parts of Southeast Asia, where illegal gambling flourishes due to inadequate enforcement and regulatory oversight. This jeopardizes player safety and deprives governments of potential tax revenues.

Ultimately, these case studies underscore the importance of tailored regulations that adapt to local contexts while embracing international standards.

You'll find that effective legislation can mitigate risks and leverage opportunities for growth in the gaming industry.

Chapter Nine

Ethics, Morality, and Social Responsibility

As you navigate the complex landscape of the gaming industry, you might find yourself questioning the ethical implications of game design and monetization strategies. With issues like gambling addiction and mental health coming to the forefront, it's essential to reflect on how social responsibility shapes the relationship between developers and players. Are current regulations truly fostering a safe and inclusive environment? And what role do transparency and accountability play in this evolving narrative? Understanding these dynamics could reveal much about the future of gaming law and its impact on everyone involved.

Ethics in game design and monetization

Ethics in game design and monetization have become essential topics as the gaming industry expands. As you navigate this landscape, you must recognize the implications of design choices and monetization strategies on player experience and behavior.

Developers often face the challenge of balancing profit motives with ethical considerations. You'll see how practices like loot boxes, microtransactions, and pay-to-win mechanics have sparked debates around fairness and transparency.

When evaluating game design, consider how certain features may exploit player psychology. For instance, using variable rewards can create addictive behaviors, leading players to spend more than intended. This raises moral questions about responsibility: Should developers prioritize engagement over player welfare?

As a player, you might appreciate well-designed experiences that respect your time and money, but not all games uphold these values.

Monetization strategies can also affect the broader gaming community. Games that prioritize ethical monetization foster goodwill, enhancing player loyalty and satisfaction. Conversely, aggressive monetization can lead to backlash, damaging a game's reputation and alienating its audience.

You should be aware of how these dynamics influence individual games and the industry.

Social responsibility for gaming companies

In an industry driven by creativity and innovation, gaming companies have a unique responsibility to contribute positively to society. This responsibility extends beyond profit-making and encompasses ethical considerations in how games are designed, marketed, and distributed. Prioritizing social responsibility can foster a more inclusive and respectful gaming environment.

One way to fulfill this responsibility is to promote diversity and representation in gaming content. By creating characters and stories that reflect a wide array of cultures, genders, and experiences, you can help combat stereotypes and encourage empathy among players. This not only enhances the gaming experience but also strengthens community ties.

Moreover, transparency in monetization practices is essential. You should avoid exploitative mechanisms targeting vulnerable audiences, particularly regarding in-game purchases. Clear communication about game costs helps build trust between you and your players, reinforcing a sense of community.

Additionally, gaming companies have the power to leverage their platforms for social change. By partnering with charitable organizations and supporting causes that resonate with your audience, you can inspire players to engage in positive actions outside the gaming world.

Ultimately, embracing social responsibility in the gaming industry isn't just a moral obligation; it's a strategic advantage. When you prioritize the well-being of your players and the broader community, you enhance your brand's reputation and contribute to a sustainable future for gaming as a whole.

Addressing gambling addiction and mental health

The gaming industry, while fostering creativity and social responsibility, must also confront the serious issue of gambling addiction and its impact on mental health. As you engage with games that involve real money, it's essential to recognize that gambling can lead to harmful behaviors and psychological distress.

Studies show that a significant percentage of gamblers experience mental health issues such as anxiety, depression, and substance abuse. The allure of winning can cloud judgment, making it easy to overlook the risks associated with gambling.

To address this, the industry needs to implement effective measures focused on prevention and support. It is important to educate players about the signs of gambling addiction and promote responsible gaming practices. This includes providing clear information about the odds of winning and tools like self-exclusion options and deposit limits.

You can make healthier choices that protect your mental well-being by fostering an informed gaming environment.

Moreover, collaboration with mental health professionals is crucial. The gaming industry should partner with organizations specializing in addiction recovery to create resources and support systems for affected individuals. Offering counseling services and helplines can provide immediate assistance and guidance.

Ultimately, addressing gambling addiction isn't solely about compliance with legal standards; it's about cultivating a culture of empathy and support. By prioritizing mental health alongside entertainment, the gaming industry can contribute to a safer and more responsible gaming experience for everyone involved.

Balancing profit and player well-being

Striking a balance between profit and player well-being poses a significant challenge for the gaming industry. On one hand, companies aim to maximize revenue through various monetization strategies, such as in-game purchases, subscriptions, and ad placements. On the other hand, these strategies can lead to negative player outcomes, including addiction and financial strain. The key lies in implementing these strategies while remaining mindful of their impact on players.

Adopting ethical practices that prioritize player engagement and satisfaction is essential to achieving this balance. By creating rewarding experiences that don't exploit players, you can foster loyalty and encourage long-term participation. This approach enhances the overall gaming experience and can lead to sustainable profit margins.

In contrast, prioritizing short-term gains may yield immediate financial benefits, but it risks damaging your brand reputation and alienating your player base.

Moreover, incorporating player feedback into game design can lead to more responsible monetization approaches. Engaging with your community allows for a better understanding of their needs and preferences, which can guide you in refining your monetization strategies. Transparency in how these strategies affect gameplay is also essential, as it builds trust between you and your players.

Ultimately, balancing profit and player well-being requires a commitment to ethical standards and a willingness to adapt to the gaming industry's evolving landscape. By prioritizing player welfare, you can create a healthier gaming environment that benefits players and your bottom line.

Transparency in advertising and game mechanics

Transparency in advertising and game mechanics is vital for building trust with players and ensuring a fair gaming experience. When game developers clearly communicate what players can expect from their products, they foster a sense of respect and loyalty.

Players deserve to know the specifics of in-game purchases, the odds of winning in loot boxes, and game mechanics that might influence their experience. Players may feel deceived without this clarity, leading to dissatisfaction and mistrust.

In the current landscape, misleading advertisements can lead to significant legal challenges. Regulatory bodies are increasingly scrutinizing claims made by game developers. For instance, if you advertise a game as having certain features later found to be exaggerated or non-existent, this damages your reputation and may result in a fine or legal action.

Moreover, understanding game mechanics is essential for informed decision-making. When developers disclose the probabilities associated with loot boxes or other random rewards, you can make educated choices about spending your money. Transparency can mitigate feelings of exploitation, particularly in games that rely on microtransactions and chance.

Ultimately, being upfront about advertising and game mechanics isn't just a legal obligation; it's a moral one. By prioritizing transparency, you can cultivate a positive relationship with your audience, promote responsible spending, and contribute to a healthier gaming environment.

Honesty is likely to attract positive responses from players, which can translate into long-term loyalty and success for your gaming projects.

Supporting diversity and inclusion in gaming

Building trust through transparency is just one aspect of creating a responsible gaming environment. Supporting diversity and inclusion in gaming is equally vital to fostering a community where all players feel valued and represented. When game developers prioritize diversity, they enrich the gaming experience and tap into a broader audience. Diverse narratives and characters resonate with players from various backgrounds, leading to increased engagement and loyalty.

Moreover, inclusive practices can enhance creativity and innovation within the industry. When teams reflect various perspectives, they're more likely to produce original concepts and address potential blind spots in game design. This diversity of thought ultimately leads to more nuanced gameplay and storytelling, which can improve player satisfaction and retention.

Incorporating diverse voices in hiring and decision-making processes is fundamental. Companies seeking talent from various demographics can cultivate an environment that values different viewpoints. This approach promotes social responsibility and aligns with evolving consumer expectations, as today's players are increasingly vocal about their desire for representation.

Furthermore, supporting diversity extends beyond the development phase. Creating inclusive gaming environments requires active efforts to guarantee that players feel safe and respected. Implementing policies that promote respectful interaction and allow for diverse expression can help achieve this goal.

Addressing sexism and harassment in online spaces

Online gaming communities can often resemble a double-edged sword, providing players with a platform for connection while simultaneously exposing them to rampant sexism and harassment.

These negative experiences can detract from gaming enjoyment, particularly for women and marginalized groups. The prevalence of toxic behavior not only creates a hostile environment but also discourages participation from those who feel threatened or unwelcome.

Addressing sexism and harassment in online spaces requires a multi-faceted approach.

First, gaming companies must implement robust reporting mechanisms that empower players to report misconduct easily and effectively. These systems should guarantee anonymity and protection against retaliation, encouraging victims to come forward without fear.

Second, fostering a culture of accountability is essential. This means that developers and community leaders should actively enforce codes of conduct and impose appropriate penalties for offenders, ranging from temporary bans to permanent account termination.

Education plays an important role in this effort. By raising awareness about the impact of harassment and sexism, you can help cultivate a more inclusive atmosphere.

Workshops, tutorials, and community discussions can serve as platforms to educate players about acceptable behavior and the importance of respect.

Promoting fairness in competitive gaming

Fairness in competitive gaming isn't just a noble ideal; it's fundamental for maintaining integrity and trust within the gaming community. When you engage in competitive gaming, you expect a level playing field where skill, strategy, and teamwork determine the outcome, not external factors. This expectation underscores the importance of promoting fairness, which can be achieved through various means.

First, transparent rules and regulations are essential. Clear guidelines help guarantee that all participants understand the expectations and limitations, reducing the potential for disputes. You should advocate for well-defined rules that apply equally to all players, regardless of their status or experience level.

Second, effective monitoring and enforcement mechanisms can help maintain fairness. Implementing systems to detect cheating, such as anti-cheat software and vigilant oversight during tournaments, reinforces the integrity of competitive play. This not only discourages dishonest behavior but also builds trust among players.

ETHICS, MORALITY, AND SOCIAL RESPONSIBILITY   139

Additionally, fostering an inclusive culture is crucial. Players from diverse backgrounds are more likely to engage positively and fairly when they feel welcomed and valued. Encouraging respectful interactions and celebrating achievements, rather than tearing down opponents, contributes to a healthier competitive environment.

Promoting fairness in competitive gaming requires a concerted effort from everyone involved—players, organizers, and developers alike. By prioritizing fairness, you help create a community that thrives on mutual respect, skill, and enjoyment, guaranteeing that competitive gaming remains a rewarding experience for all participants.

Regulations on violent and graphic content

In gaming, regulations on violent and graphic content play an essential role in shaping player experiences and industry standards. These regulations aim to balance artistic expression with social responsibility, protecting players from potentially harmful material. Various organizations, including the Entertainment Software Rating Board (ESRB) and Pan European Game Information (PEGI), evaluate games based on their content, assigning ratings that inform consumers and parents about the nature of the material.

You'll notice that these ratings help guide your choices as a player or a guardian, clarifying what's appropriate for different age groups. For instance, a game designated for mature audiences may contain graphic violence or explicit themes, which could influence your decision to engage with that content.

The implications of these regulations extend beyond individual choices; they also shape industry practices. Developers often adjust their content to align with regulatory standards, as non-compliance can lead to financial penalties or reputational damage.

Moreover, public sentiment plays a significant role in shaping these regulations. Social movements advocating for responsible gaming often push for stricter guidelines, reflecting concerns about the impact of violent content on society.

This dynamic relationship between regulation, industry practices, and public opinion highlights the importance of maintaining a dialogue about what constitutes acceptable content in gaming. In this evolving landscape, understanding these regulations empowers you to make informed decisions about your gaming experiences while considering the broader implications for society.

Community guidelines and moderation practices

Community guidelines and moderation practices are essential for fostering safe and engaging gaming environments. They create a framework that helps you navigate the complexities of online interactions, ensuring your experience is enjoyable while minimizing harmful behavior. By implementing clear guidelines, gaming companies can encourage positive player interactions and discourage toxicity.

Effective community guidelines should address various aspects of player behavior, including:

- **Respect**: Promoting a culture where every player feels valued and acknowledged.

- **Inclusivity**: Ensuring that diverse voices are welcomed, creating a richer gaming experience.

- **Accountability**: Holding players responsible for their actions, reinforcing the importance of respectful communication.

- **Safety**: Protecting players from harassment and abusive behavior, allowing them to engage without fear.

- **Constructive Feedback**: Encouraging players to voice their opinions while maintaining respect and civility.

Moderation practices play a crucial role in enforcing these guidelines. They involve monitoring player interactions, responding to reports of misconduct, and applying appropriate consequences when necessary.

An effective moderation team upholds the standards outlined in the community guidelines and actively engages with players, fostering a sense of belonging and trust.

As the gaming industry evolves, the significance of these practices can't be overstated. They're not just about enforcing rules but about building a community where everyone can thrive.

Responsible use of player data and analytics

With the rise of data-driven decision-making in the gaming industry, the responsible use of player data and analytics has become a significant concern. You must understand the implications of collecting and utilizing player data as a developer or operator. This information can enhance user experience and improve game design, but it also raises ethical questions about privacy, consent, and data security.

You should prioritize transparency in your data practices. Clearly communicate to players what data you're collecting, how you're using it, and for what purpose. This builds trust and guarantees players feel respected and valued.

Consent is another essential aspect; obtaining explicit permission before collecting personal data is not only ethical but often legally required.

Data security is equally important. Implement robust safeguards to protect player information from breaches and unauthorized access. A single data leak can damage your reputation and lead to legal repercussions.

Moreover, consider the implications of analytics regarding player behavior. Using data to exploit vulnerabilities or manipulate spending habits can lead to harmful practices. Endeavor uses analytics to foster a healthy gaming environment that promotes engagement without taking advantage of players.

Ultimately, responsible data use isn't just about compliance; it reflects your commitment to ethical standards within the gaming community. You can contribute to a gaming culture that values innovation and integrity by prioritizing player rights and ethical practices.

Regulatory push for "safe" gaming spaces

The gaming industry is witnessing a growing regulatory push to create "safe" gaming spaces for players. This movement is largely driven by concerns around addiction, mental health, and the overall well-being of gamers. You might find it striking how regulations are evolving to guarantee that gaming environments promote responsible behavior and protect vulnerable populations.

Consider these critical factors that underline the importance of safe gaming spaces:

- **Preventing addiction**: Regulations seek to mitigate risks associated with excessive gaming, guaranteeing players don't lose control.

- **Mental health support**: Encouraging developers to incorporate features that promote well-being, such as breaks and wellness reminders.

- **Transparency**: Establishing clear communication about in-game purchases and mechanics to avoid misleading players.

- **Age verification**: Enforcing stricter controls guarantees that underage individuals aren't exposed to inappropriate content.

- **Community guidelines**: Fostering a supportive online environment where harassment and toxic behavior are actively discouraged.

As these regulations gain momentum, you'll notice that they aim to protect players and encourage developers to adopt ethical practices.

Compliance with these regulations could ultimately enhance the gaming industry's reputation, leading to a more positive relationship between developers and players.

The focus on creating safe gaming spaces reflects a broader societal responsibility. It advocates for an industry that values the health and safety of its community while fostering a culture of accountability.

Parental controls and child protection policies

As the gaming industry increasingly focuses on creating safe environments for players, parental controls and child protection policies have become integral components of this effort. These tools aim to empower parents, allowing them to regulate their children's gaming experiences while protecting them from potential online dangers.

Parental controls typically enable you to set limits on screen time, restrict access to certain content, and monitor your child's interactions in multiplayer environments. Using these features, you can tailor your child's gaming experience to align with your family's values and guarantee age-appropriate content.

Moreover, many platforms now provide resources and guides to help you navigate these settings effectively.

Child protection policies within the gaming industry also play an essential role in safeguarding young players. These policies often include measures such as reporting systems for inappropriate behavior, strict age verification processes, and guidelines for developers to follow.

By enforcing these standards, the industry aims to create a more secure gaming environment where children can enjoy their experiences without fear of exploitation or harmful interactions.

However, you must remain vigilant and engaged in your child's gaming habits. Open communication about online safety and responsible gaming practices is significant, even with robust parental controls and policies.

This collaborative approach helps you foster a safe and enjoyable gaming journey for your child, guaranteeing they can explore the digital world while minimizing risks.

Environmental impact of gaming hardware

Examining the environmental impact of gaming hardware reveals significant concerns regarding sustainability and resource consumption. As a gamer, you mightn't consider the broader implications of your gaming setup, but the reality is that the production and disposal of gaming hardware contribute to environmental degradation.

Here's a closer look at some critical issues:

- **E-waste**: Millions of tons of electronic waste are generated annually, often ending up in landfills where toxic substances leach into the soil and water.

- **Resource depletion**: The extraction of minerals used in manufacturing components, such as rare earth metals, leads to habitat destruction and biodiversity loss.

- **Energy consumption**: Gaming consoles and PCs consume substantial amounts of electricity, contributing to higher carbon footprints, especially if powered by fossil fuels.

- **Plastic pollution**: Packaging and components often contain non-biodegradable plastics, which persist in the environment for centuries.

- **Short product lifecycles**: Rapid technological advancements encourage a culture of obsolescence, pushing consumers to frequently upgrade, thereby exacerbating waste.

To mitigate these impacts, you can adopt more sustainable practices. Consider investing in energy-efficient hardware, recycling old devices, and advocating for companies to prioritize eco-friendly materials and production processes.

The ethical future of gaming law

Steering the ethical future of gaming law requires a careful balance between innovation and responsibility. As technology evolves, so do the complexities of legal frameworks surrounding gaming, including issues like user data protection, intellectual property rights, and the regulation of in-game economies.

You must consider how these laws can adapt to the rapid pace of change while ensuring fair treatment for all stakeholders, from developers to players.

One of the primary challenges you'll face is the potential for exploitation within microtransactions and loot boxes. These elements can blur the lines between entertainment and gambling, raising ethical questions about consumer protection.

As you navigate these waters, you must advocate for transparent regulations prioritizing player welfare without stifling creativity and business growth.

Moreover, the rise of online gaming and esports introduces new dimensions regarding harassment and discrimination, necessitating robust legal protections.

You'll need to champion inclusive environments and advocate for laws that penalize toxic behavior and promote positive community standards.

Finally, as gaming increasingly intersects with issues like mental health and social responsibility, you should engage in an ongoing dialogue about the implications of gaming on society.

This includes evaluating content regulation and age restrictions and ensuring that laws evolve alongside societal norms.

Chapter Ten

Future Legal Challenges in Gaming

As you navigate the rapidly evolving gaming landscape, you'll notice that future legal challenges are becoming more complex and nuanced. With the rise of decentralized platforms and immersive technologies, the legal frameworks governing intellectual property, data privacy, and player protection must adapt. You might question how current regulations will hold up against user-generated content and the potential for new monetization strategies. What implications will these changes have for developers and players alike, and how can you prepare for the unforeseen legal intricacies that lie ahead?

The rise of the metaverse and virtual worlds

As we venture into the digital age, the rise of the metaverse and virtual worlds has transformed how we interact, socialize, and conduct business. These immersive environments enable you to create avatars, attend events, and engage in commerce in previously unimaginable ways.

The blend of augmented reality (AR) and virtual reality (VR) technologies allows for a seamless experience, making it feel like you're truly present in the digital domain. This evolution isn't just about gaming; it's reshaping social interactions and business models across various sectors.

In the metaverse, you can participate in virtual economies, buying and selling digital goods using cryptocurrencies or in-game tokens. This shift has led to new opportunities for creators and entrepreneurs who can innovatively monetize their skills and ideas.

However, it also raises questions about ownership, value, and the implications of a decentralized economy. For instance, what happens to your virtual assets if the hosting platform shuts down?

Moreover, the social dynamics of virtual worlds complicate traditional paradigms of interaction. You're not merely a spectator; you're an active participant in communities that span the globe.

This interconnectedness fosters collaboration but can also lead to privacy, data security, and personal conduct challenges. As these virtual spaces continue to grow, understanding their implications for social and economic interactions will be essential for stakeholders in the gaming industry.

Legal challenges in decentralized platforms

While decentralized platforms offer innovative solutions for digital interaction and commerce, they also present many legal challenges that can complicate their operation. One key issue revolves around regulatory compliance. Determining which jurisdiction's laws apply can be tricky without a central authority. You might find yourself maneuvering through a patchwork of regulations that vary widely between regions, creating uncertainty for both developers and users.

Another challenge lies in intellectual property rights. In decentralized environments, content can be easily replicated and distributed without proper authorization, leading to potential copyright infringements. You may struggle to enforce your rights effectively, as traditional legal frameworks may not adequately address the unique characteristics of these platforms.

Additionally, issues of accountability arise. Identifying and prosecuting an individual can be nearly impossible if a user engages in illegal activities on a decentralized platform. This situation raises questions about liability—who's responsible when harm occurs? The decentralized nature often obscures the trail of accountability, complicating legal recourse.

Moreover, you must consider user data protection. With decentralized platforms frequently collecting personal information, ensuring compliance with data privacy laws like GDPR becomes essential. Failure to do so can lead to significant fines and reputational damage.

The future of IP in digital-only assets

In the coming years, the landscape of intellectual property (IP) in digital-only assets is poised for significant evolution. As more gamers engage with virtual goods, NFTs, and other digital properties, the legal frameworks surrounding these assets must adapt to new realities.

Here are four key aspects to take into account:

1. **Ownership Rights**: As digital assets become more prevalent, defining ownership will be vital. You'll need to understand how blockchain technology impacts ownership rights and what that means for creators and consumers.

2. **Licensing Agreements**: With the rise of user-generated content,

the way you create and share digital assets will necessitate clearer licensing agreements. You'll want to ensure these agreements protect your interests while fostering innovation.

3. **Enforcement Challenges**: As digital assets often cross borders, enforcing IP rights can become complex. You may face challenges in jurisdiction and enforcement, requiring a more global approach to IP protection.

4. **Evolving Regulations**: Expect to see emerging regulations around digital assets. Governments will likely implement new laws to address the unique characteristics of digital-only assets, so staying informed will be critical.

Navigating these changes will require vigilance and adaptability. As the IP landscape evolves, you'll need to be proactive in understanding your rights and responsibilities, ensuring that you protect your creations and contribute positively to the gaming ecosystem.

Cybersecurity and player protection

Cybersecurity has become a significant concern in the gaming industry as threats to player data and in-game assets continue to escalate. You're likely aware that breaches can lead to substantial financial losses for players, developers, and publishers. Personal information, such as credit card details or login credentials, erodes trust and can affect a game's reputation when compromised.

To mitigate these risks, gaming companies must implement robust cybersecurity measures. This includes encryption protocols that protect data during transmission, multi-factor authentication to bolster account security, and regular vulnerability assessments to identify potential weaknesses in their systems.

It's also essential for developers to stay informed about emerging threats, such as ransomware or phishing attacks, which are increasingly targeting online gaming platforms.

Moreover, player education plays an important role in enhancing security. You should know the importance of using strong, unique passwords and recognizing suspicious activities. Game developers can assist by providing clear guidelines on how to protect personal information and encouraging players to report any irregularities they encounter.

Regulatory bodies are likely to impose stricter requirements on cybersecurity practices in the gaming industry, emphasizing the need for compliance. As a player, you have the right to expect a secure environment for your gaming experience.

Balancing innovative game design with stringent security protocols is essential, ensuring that player protection remains a priority in an ever-evolving digital landscape.

Anticipating regulatory changes for VR/AR

The rapid evolution of VR and AR technologies is prompting a wave of regulatory scrutiny aimed at safeguarding users and ensuring ethical practices. As these immersive experiences become more integrated into daily life, you should anticipate several regulatory changes that could reshape the VR and AR gaming landscape.

1. **User Privacy Protections**: Expect enhanced regulations around data collection and user consent. With VR and AR systems often gathering extensive personal data, lawmakers will likely impose stricter guidelines to protect user information.

2. **Content Regulation**: As VR and AR content can blur the lines between reality and fiction, regulatory bodies may introduce rules governing harmful or misleading content. This could include age restrictions and content ratings similar to traditional media.

3. **Intellectual Property Rights**: As creators develop unique VR and AR experiences, the need for clearer intellectual property laws will arise. You might see new frameworks designed to protect innovations while balancing fair use.

4. **Health and Safety Standards**: Ongoing concerns about the physical and psychological impacts of VR and AR use could lead to mandatory health and safety guidelines. These may cover everything from the duration of use to designing user interfaces that minimize strain and discomfort.

Navigating these potential changes requires staying informed and prepared as regulatory landscapes evolve to keep pace with technological advancements.

Predicting trends in online gambling laws

As technology continues to reshape various sectors, online gambling laws are also poised for significant changes. One trend you'll likely notice is the increasing push for regulatory harmonization across jurisdictions. As more countries recognize the economic benefits of legalized online gambling, you can expect a concerted effort to create consistent frameworks that govern this industry. This could lead to a more standardized approach, simplifying operators' compliance and protecting consumers more effectively.

FUTURE LEGAL CHALLENGES IN GAMING 153

Another trend is the growing emphasis on responsible gambling measures. As online platforms become more accessible, regulators will likely mandate operators implement enhanced safeguards. This includes features like self-exclusion tools and deposit limits, aimed at minimizing the risks of gambling addiction. You'll find that these regulations cannot only enhance player safety but also bolster the industry's credibility.

Moreover, the rise of mobile gaming is pushing lawmakers to rethink their strategies. With more players engaging through smartphones, regulations tailored to mobile platforms may address issues like geolocation and age verification more rigorously. This evolution will require operators to adapt quickly, ensuring they remain compliant while attracting a diverse user base.

Lastly, data privacy regulations will be essential in shaping online gambling laws. Given the vast amounts of personal data collected, lawmakers will likely impose stringent requirements on how this information is handled.

Blockchain and tokenization in gaming

How is blockchain technology transforming the gaming landscape? Blockchain is revolutionizing how you interact with games and in-game assets. Players gain greater ownership and control over their digital items by utilizing decentralized ledgers. Tokenization, a core principle of blockchain, allows the creation of unique digital assets that can be traded or sold, fundamentally changing the gaming economy.

Here are four key ways blockchain and tokenization impact gaming:
1. **True Ownership**: Unlike traditional games, where developers retain control over assets, blockchain enables you to own your items outright. You can buy, sell, or trade them freely, creating a

player-driven economy.

2. **Interoperability**: Tokenized assets can be used across different games and platforms, enhancing the gaming experience. For example, a unique sword could be utilized in multiple games, increasing its value and utility.

3. **Transparency and Security**: Blockchain's transparent nature protects you from fraud. Every transaction is recorded on an immutable ledger, ensuring that the provenance of your assets is verifiable.

4. **Decentralized Economies**: With blockchain, you can participate in decentralized marketplaces where you set the price for your assets. This empowers you, the player, to dictate the economy rather than relying on developers or publishers.

As blockchain technology evolves, the gaming industry must adapt to these changes, presenting opportunities and challenges in legal frameworks and regulations.

Impacts of AI on gaming law evolution

AI's rapid advancement is markedly reshaping the legal landscape of gaming. As you explore this evolution, you'll notice that AI technologies are enhancing game design and player experiences and introducing complex legal challenges.

For instance, AI's ability to analyze player behavior raises questions about data privacy and consent. You must comprehend how laws must adapt to protect personal information while allowing developers to leverage AI for improved gaming experiences.

Moreover, AI's role in creating dynamic in-game environments leads to issues around intellectual property rights. When AI generates unique content, who owns that content? This ambiguity could lead to disputes and necessitate re-evaluating existing copyright laws. As a legal professional, you must navigate these murky waters and advocate for clear guidelines.

Additionally, the use of AI in gaming can influence gambling laws. AI-driven predictive algorithms could impact responsible gaming practices, prompting regulators to enact legislation to guarantee player protection. Balancing innovation with consumer safety is a delicate task that requires ongoing dialogue among stakeholders.

Lastly, AI's potential to automate game testing and debugging processes suggests a shift in liability considerations. If an AI system causes a defect in a game, who's responsible? As AI continues to integrate into gaming, you'll need to stay informed and proactive about how these advancements require rethinking legal frameworks to guarantee fair play and accountability.

Role of international bodies in standardizing laws

The increasing complexity of gaming laws, exacerbated by advancements in AI, underscores the need for a unified global approach to regulation. You might wonder how international bodies can contribute to standardizing these laws, especially when disparate regulations hinder the industry's growth and innovation.

These organizations can help mitigate legal discrepancies across borders by establishing clear guidelines.

Here are four key roles international bodies can play:

1. **Harmonization of Regulations**: They can work towards creating a cohesive framework that aligns various national laws, making compliance easier for gaming companies operating in multiple jurisdictions.

2. **Best Practices Development**: By sharing insights and data, international bodies can formulate best practices that promote responsible gaming, consumer protection, and fair competition.

3. **Dispute Resolution Mechanisms**: They can establish impartial mechanisms for resolving disputes arising from international gaming activities, ensuring fairness and transparency for all parties involved.

4. **Advocacy and Education**: These organizations can advocate for effective legislation that reflects the evolving nature of gaming and educate stakeholders on compliance and regulatory updates.

Privacy and AI-enhanced personalization

Maneuvering the intersection of privacy and AI-enhanced gaming personalization presents opportunities and challenges. As a developer or stakeholder in the gaming industry, you're likely aware that AI can notably enhance user experiences by tailoring content to individual preferences. However, this personalization often requires extensive data collection, raising critical privacy concerns.

When you implement AI systems that analyze player behavior, you gather vast amounts of sensitive data. This data can include personal identifiers, gameplay habits, and even in-game purchases. While this information can help you create a more engaging gaming environment, it also puts you at risk of violating privacy laws, such as the General Data Protection Regulation (GDPR) or the California Consumer Privacy Act (CCPA).

Guiding through these regulations isn't just a matter of compliance; it's about building trust with your players. You must confirm that players know what data you collect and how it's used. Transparent communication is key. Implementing user-friendly privacy settings allows players to control their data, fostering a sense of security.

Additionally, anonymizing data can mitigate risks while still enabling personalized experiences. Balancing personalization with privacy isn't just a legal obligation; it's essential for sustaining player engagement and loyalty.

As you innovate with AI, consider the ethical implications and aim to prioritize your players' privacy. By doing so, you comply with regulations and enhance your brand's reputation in an increasingly privacy-conscious market.

Preparing for regulation in immersive tech

Maneuvering the evolving landscape of immersive technology requires a proactive approach to regulation. Understanding the regulatory environment is essential as you develop and implement immersive tech in gaming. Here's how you can prepare effectively:

1. **Stay Informed on Current Legislation**: Review existing laws related to data protection, user privacy, and content regulation regularly. This knowledge helps you anticipate potential changes that could impact your operations.

2. **Engage with Regulatory Bodies**: Establish open lines of com-

munication with local and international regulatory agencies. By engaging with these entities, you can provide input on emerging regulations and gain insights into future regulatory trends.

3. **Implement Robust Compliance Frameworks**: Develop compliance programs that align with existing regulations. By instilling a culture of compliance within your organization, you can mitigate legal risks while fostering trust with users.

4. **Monitor Technological Advancements**: Monitor technological developments in immersive tech. As innovations arise, they may prompt new regulations or require adjustments to existing ones. Staying ahead guarantees compliance and competitiveness.

Preparing for regulation in immersive tech isn't just about adhering to laws; it's about fostering an environment of ethical innovation.

Potential changes to age restriction laws

As discussions around gaming regulations evolve, you may find that potential changes to age restriction laws become increasingly significant. Currently, age restrictions in gaming are often based on the game's content. Still, there's a growing conversation about how these laws should adapt to the rapidly changing gaming industry landscape.

With younger audiences engaging more with complex narratives and multiplayer online experiences, you'll need to reflect on the implications of these shifts. One significant factor is the rise of user-generated content, which can blur the lines of appropriateness.

Games like Roblox and Fortnite allow players to create and share their content, raising questions about how age restrictions are enforced. Regulators may need to re-evaluate their criteria to account for the unpredictable nature of user-generated environments.

Moreover, the increasing prevalence of mobile gaming means that access is easier than ever for young players. This could prompt lawmakers to implement stricter guidelines, potentially leading to a more standardized approach across different platforms and devices.

You should also be aware of the ongoing debates surrounding the effectiveness of current age rating systems, such as the ESRB or PEGI, which some argue don't sufficiently protect minors from inappropriate content.

As you navigate this evolving landscape, you must stay informed about legislative actions and industry responses. The future of age restriction laws in gaming will likely reflect technological advancements and societal attitudes toward youth engagement in interactive media.

Future of loot boxes and gambling regulations

With age restrictions being scrutinized more closely, the conversation naturally extends to the future of loot boxes and gambling regulations in gaming.

You'll find that legislators worldwide are looking closer at how loot boxes function, especially concerning their potential to encourage gambling behaviors among younger players. As you navigate this evolving landscape, consider the following key points:

1. **Definition Clarity**: Regulatory bodies are working towards a clearer definition of loot boxes compared to traditional gambling, which will impact how these mechanisms are categorized legally.

2. **Disclosure Requirements**: Game developers will likely be required to disclose the odds of obtaining specific items in loot

boxes, similar to regulations seen in markets like Japan and China.

3. **Age Restrictions**: You can expect more stringent age restrictions imposed on games featuring loot boxes, aiming to protect minors from potential gambling addiction.

4. **Potential Taxation**: Governments might explore taxing loot box sales, treating them similarly to gambling revenue, which could lead to a significant financial shift within the gaming industry.

These developments indicate a future where loot boxes could face substantial regulations, forcing game developers to adapt their monetization strategies.

Staying informed about these changes is essential for anyone involved in the gaming industry, as they could reshape how you create and market games.

Protecting game developers and creators

In recent years, the gaming industry has faced many legal challenges that threaten developers' and creators' creative freedom and financial stability.

As a game developer, you must understand the importance of protecting your intellectual property. Copyright issues are rampant, with many games being cloned or modified without permission. You must take proactive steps to secure your creations through proper registration and monitoring for potential infringements.

Additionally, consider the implications of contracts and agreements you enter into. Clear, enforceable contracts with publishers and collaborators can safeguard your interests. You'll want to guarantee that the terms regarding revenue sharing, ownership rights, and liability are well-defined to avoid future disputes.

Moreover, the rise of user-generated content poses unique challenges. While you might be excited about players creating mods or fan art, be cautious.

Establishing clear guidelines on how fans can use your intellectual property is essential. This will not only protect your work but also foster a positive community.

Envisioning gaming law 20 years from now

Two decades from now, the future of gaming law is likely to be shaped by rapid technological advancements and evolving societal norms. As a gamer and industry stakeholder, you must navigate a legal landscape that reflects these changes.

Here are four key areas you can expect to see significant evolution:

1. **Intellectual Property Rights**: As games become more immersive and community-driven, the definitions of ownership and copyright must adapt. Expect clearer guidelines on user-generated content and its commercial use.

2. **Data Privacy and Security**: With the rise of virtual reality and pervasive data collection, regulations surrounding player data will tighten. Companies must comply with stricter standards to protect users' information, which will affect how you engage online.

3. **Esports Regulations**: As esports gains mainstream acceptance, you'll notice formalized structures around player rights, contracts, and tournament regulations. This will lead to fairer treatment and increased professionalism within competitive gaming.

4. **Microtransactions and Loot Boxes**: Legal scrutiny over monetization strategies will intensify. Governments will likely implement clearer regulations to protect consumers, especially minors, from predatory practices.

In essence, the gaming industry must adapt proactively to these legal challenges.

Conclusion

Today's gaming industry is a fascinating and pivotal intersection of innovation, law, and ethics. What began as a niche form of entertainment has evolved into a global, multi-billion-dollar ecosystem that touches nearly every aspect of modern society, from technology and culture to finance and public policy. As gaming expands into new formats, from virtual reality and blockchain to eSports and mobile gaming, so does its legal landscape's complexity. *The Law of Play* has explored these dimensions, equipping stakeholders—developers, players, investors, and regulators—with essential knowledge to navigate the challenges and responsibilities of operating in this unique space. In conclusion, it's clear that understanding the legalities in gaming isn't just about compliance; it's about fostering a balanced environment where creativity, fairness, and accountability can coexist.

A Sector Defined by Rapid Change and Complexity

The rapid pace of technological advancement in gaming has created a continuously evolving landscape, with new challenges arising just as quickly as they are resolved. The development of immersive technologies, like virtual and augmented reality, has transformed gameplay experiences and brought legal questions surrounding data privacy, safety, and psychological effects to the forefront. Similarly, the growth of blockchain and decentralized gaming platforms has opened avenues for players to "own" digital assets in ways never before possible, introducing unique questions about intellectual property, ownership rights, and security.

These changes are far-reaching, affecting how games are made and played and how they are regulated. Policymakers and regulators must constantly adapt to the shifting dynamics within the gaming ecosystem, working to create laws that protect consumers without stifling innovation. This balance is no easy task, especially as gaming technologies push the boundaries of what's possible in both gameplay and business models. However, recognizing these trends and understanding the legal principles that apply enables stakeholders to make better decisions, anticipate risks, and seize opportunities as they arise.

Legal Knowledge as a Tool for Empowerment

For game developers and publishers, legal knowledge is a foundation for making informed choices that respect player rights and business interests. By understanding licensing requirements, intellectual property laws, and the intricacies of monetization models, companies can avoid costly legal disputes, foster consumer trust, and uphold their brand integrity. Compliance with these regulations is not merely an obligation; it's a path to sustainable success in a field where consumer expectations and regulatory demands are constantly evolving.

Understanding their rights within games and the protections afforded to them by law empowers players to demand fairness, transparency, and accountability from gaming companies. Players today are increasingly informed about practices like loot boxes, microtransactions, and data collection, and they have the tools to make choices that align with their values and preferences. From privacy regulations to consumer rights, legal protections help maintain a fair playing field, giving players confidence that their data, investments, and experiences are safeguarded.

For investors and stakeholders, grasping the regulatory environment is critical to assessing risks and opportunities in gaming ventures. With the rapid growth of eSports, the integration of virtual goods, and the use of cryptocurrency in gaming transactions, the financial aspects of the industry are more interconnected with legal considerations than ever before. Investors must weigh the potential rewards of this lucrative sector against the regulatory risks that come with it, including jurisdictional complexities, international compliance, and shifts in public sentiment toward certain gaming practices. Knowledge of gaming law not only mitigates potential pitfalls but can also illuminate the best paths for responsible and profitable investments.

The Role of Ethics and Social Responsibility

Beyond the technicalities of regulation, gaming law is increasingly shaped by ethical and social concerns. The industry's responsibility to promote fair play, protect vulnerable users, and foster inclusive communities cannot be understated. Gaming companies have a significant influence on their audiences, and this power comes with the duty to protect users from harm, respect privacy, and ensure transparency in-game mechanics and monetization.

Socially responsible practices are ethically imperative and beneficial for long-term brand loyalty and public trust. In an era where players and regulators are holding companies accountable, ethics in gaming are more important than ever. Whether addressing gambling addiction through age restrictions, mitigating exposure to harmful content, or protecting minors in online spaces, ethical considerations guide the industry toward safer and more inclusive environments. By adopting best practices and being proactive in ethical matters, gaming companies demonstrate a commitment to their users beyond profit motives.

Anticipating the Future of Gaming Law

As the gaming industry moves forward, several emerging trends will likely shape its legal landscape. The growth of the metaverse, for example, brings with it new questions about virtual property rights, user identity, and cross-platform interoperability. Likewise, as artificial intelligence continues to be integrated into game development, issues surrounding data protection, automated moderation, and algorithmic transparency are set to become even more prominent. These developments demand regulators, companies, and users stay agile, proactive, and open to adapting as the industry evolves.

Internationally, the push for harmonized gaming regulations could create more consistency across borders, potentially making it easier for gaming companies to operate globally. However, the cultural and legal differences among countries remain challenging, as seen in the varied approaches to issues like loot boxes and online gambling. Cross-border cooperation will likely grow as gaming becomes increasingly globalized, but companies must continue to account for the regional nuances that influence how laws are applied.

With the rise of digital assets, NFTs, and virtual economies, intellectual property law will play an even greater role in shaping gaming's future. Protecting these assets becomes critical as players invest real money in virtual items. Game developers must develop policies that respect player ownership while safeguarding their creative rights, ensuring that both parties have legal clarity in this new paradigm.

Closing Thoughts: Navigating the Rules of Play

The legal landscape of the gaming industry is complex yet fascinating. Rapid innovation and regulatory oversight converge to create a unique set of challenges and opportunities. The journey through *The Law of Play* underscores the importance of legal knowledge for all stakeholders involved in the industry. By understanding the rules governing gaming, stakeholders are better prepared to create, invest in, or enjoy gaming experiences that are both legally sound but also fair and ethical.

This book aims to provide a comprehensive foundation, covering the broad spectrum of legalities that impact the industry—from licensing and intellectual property to monetization models, consumer protections, and the ethical dimensions of game design. Yet, new legal questions and ethical dilemmas will arise as the gaming industry continues to expand and intersect with other sectors. Remaining vigilant, adaptable, and informed will be essential for everyone engaged in gaming's evolving landscape.

Ultimately, gaming law is more than regulation; it is about cultivating an industry that respects creativity, protects players, and encourages responsible innovation. For developers, this means building games that balance engagement with transparency; for regulators, it means crafting policies that protect consumers without stifling growth; and for players, it means knowing their rights and holding companies to high standards. As we look to the future of gaming, we see a space rich with potential—a world where play, law, and ethics can harmoniously coexist.

The rules of play will continue to evolve. With the knowledge and insights gained from *The Law of Play*, you are now equipped to navigate them, ensuring that every level you reach in the industry is grounded in legality, fairness, and a vision for a responsible gaming future.